THE HIDDEN KINGDO

According to Buddhist
subterranean land lo
centre of our plan
believe that mi
undergroun
destinies ar and
all-wise ruler, w as 'the
King of the World.
The Buddhist religion the oldest and
most sophisticated in the d. So is the story
of Agharta nothing more than fable – or is
there truth behind the legend?

Many peoples of different religions have strongly believed in a world within our world. Today, for example, many respected seekers after truth firmly maintain that the 'lost' civilization of Atlantis lives on beneath the Earth's surface.

How many of these subterranean worlds really exist . . . ?

This Hollow Earth

WARREN SMITH

SPHERE BOOKS LIMITED
30/32 Gray's Inn Road, London WC1X 8JL

First published in Great Britain by Sphere Books Ltd 1977

To My Son, Steve
And all others who believe in myths,
magic, and mystery.

Set in Linotype Pilgrim

Printed in Great Britain by
Hazell Watson & Viney Ltd
Aylesbury, Bucks

THE WEIRD WORLD INSIDE THE HOLLOW EARTH

Like some veiled demon conjured up by a black magician, the belief in a hollow earth is one of the most intriguing of the various occult mysteries.

The hollow earth theory is a mind-shattering proposal that there are gigantic holes at the north and south poles. These polar openings lead to a vast, unknown world inside the center of the earth. Some believers also claim the earth is honeycombed with a vast network of subterranean tunnels that lead down to the inner world.

If that isn't enough to boggle your mind, hollow earth enthusiasts declare that these interior lands are inhabited by giants, fairies, 'the wee people,' demonic animal-men, or a race of gentle, advanced people. Depending on who you are talking to, these benign inhabitants inside the earth are said to be the survivors of Atlantis, Lemuria, or an unknown race. Certain UFOlogists have theorized that flying saucers originate from the hollow earth, piloted by intra-terrestrials from these subterranean worlds.

'The Masters dwell in the paradise inside the earth,' reported one believer. 'Their mission is to guide surface *homo sapiens* to higher spirituality. Surface man is polluting the entire planet. Our atomic explosions have endangered the environment of the inner earth. The Masters are disturbed because we cannot live peacefully in the outer world.'

Other believers are not so certain that the land within the earth is inhabited by a calm, cultured society of wise men. They whisper about the deadly 'dero' – detrimental robots – bloodthirsty half men, half animals, who are endowed with deadly powers and dark lusts.

'Deros create most of the problems found in the surface world,' declared another hollow earth believer. 'They get a sadistic delight in torturing, murdering, and kidnapping men and women. They cause our wars, create diseases and plagues, and they sabotage machinery to cause car, plane, and train crashes.'

A German industrialist sat quietly in his office one afternoon and talked seriously of Adolf Hitler's belief in a hollow earth. 'Hitler was obsessed with reaching these new lands,' the manufacturer reported. 'The *Thule Society*, Hitler's beliefs, and the black monks of the swastika order were behind the Third Reich and Hitler's rise to power.'

Like many theories that are primarily based on legends, folk lore, and mythology, the hollow earth mystery is spiced with tales of sexual encounters between surface women and the demonic deros, tunnel creatures, and devilmen. Some hollow earth enthusiasts claim these weird beings sate their unbridled lust by kidnapping young girls and attractive women. The terror-stricken victims are dragged down into the smoky caverns, locked in breeding pens, and assaulted by the monsters.

'Young girls and women are disappearing at an alarming rate throughout the world,' said a solemn-faced believer. 'In Italy, these missing women are said to be the victims of a treacherous ring of white slavers. In India, a nation that is a hot-bed of dero activity, the missing girls are alleged to have been impressed into Italian convents. In Europe and America, the authorities blame the drug culture and runaways from home. I believe that the deros are on the march again. They are filling their breeding cages with their female victims!'

Cultists who believe that the Under-People are benign, gentle, and endowed with ancient wisdom, have also created another sexual theory.

'Female Under-People are beautiful,' said the president of the Hollow Earth Society. 'They are the most attractive, most graceful, women in the universe. Check your mythology and history; you'll discover that certain men have been guided by Goddess-like women. The ancient Greeks and Romans established an entire theology on these beings. Their Gods and Goddesses were emissaries from the hollow earth. Sexual contact between these advanced people and ordinary *homo sapiens* brought forth the Advanced Man, beings who were far superior physically and mentally to their peers.'

Whether you believe in a hollow earth, benign beings, or demonic deros, will depend on your personal attitudes. Several aspects of the mystery are worth investigation because of the long history of this persistent belief. Humanity has always sought an answer to the size, shape, composition, history, and universal significance of our planet. Admittedly, a large portion of our world has been methodically explored, mapped, plotted, and surveyed. Yet, despite the magnificent efforts of our ancestors, and our increasing technology, there are many 'unknown' areas on a world atlas.

Our pioneer astronauts have journeyed to the moon and brought back samples of lunar rock and dust. Yet, as we soar into space, we have no knowledge of the myriad secrets hidden beneath the waters of the world's oceans. Do sunken continents rest on the bottoms of the oceans? Do the waves crest over sunken cities? Hollow earth believers point out that few men have ventured into the dense wilderness of the Brazilian jungles; those who penetrate the jungles frequently return with stories and photographs of lost cities and mysterious ruins.

In recent years, pyramids have been discovered throughout the world. Massive pyramids, dead cities, and gigantic subterranean lakes are reported from the unexplored areas of Asia. No one can foretell what may be discovered in the cloistered valleys of the Himalayan mountains. The barren deserts of the world have not yielded their treasure trove of data on man's enigmatic past. The north and south polar regions are covered with snow and ice, shrouded in cold, and veiled in mystery.

In the pages that follow, you will read some wild, far-out

claims. The material can be judged according to your beliefs. It can be dismissed as pseudo-science or a misinterpretation of normal planetary phenomena. Those who claim to have met the Under-People can be judged as individuals with mental aberrations. You may conclude that the hollow earth theory is simply semi-factual science fiction. Or, you may decide that the hollow earth believers have based their case solidly on fact.

'In a changing world where almost any event can occur with frightening suddenness, we may arise some morning to learn that our governments have contacted the inhabitants of the inner lands,' believers stated.

If, as some scientists have suggested, the moon is hollow, then our own planet could conceivably be pregnant with undiscovered lands, subterranean cities, and unknown people. According to the Hollow Earth Society, there is evidence throughout history of men who accidentally learned of this subterranean world.

'A few of these people managed to return to the surface world,' claimed Albert McDonald, president of the Hollow Earth Society. 'No one bothered to actually check their stories. These men were ridiculed, harassed, and frequently placed in the lunatic ward of the nearest asylum.'

UFOs from the Inner Land

Until recently, the world's occultists simply dismissed the hollow earth theory as the misguided rantings of ignorant cultists. However, over the past few years, sightings of Unidentified Flying Objects and the antics of their occupants have mystified both official and civilian investigators. Several civilian UFO organizations established strict guidelines concerning this space age mystery. They clung to the belief that UFOs originated from another planet in outer space. Yet, accounts of UFO occupants or pilots were summarily dismissed as unbelievable. Despite criticism for their views, a small group of UFO researchers adopted an open-minded, admittedly sometimes far-out, approach to the origin of UFOs.

These 'far-out' hypotheses included the possibility that UFOs and their occupants were from other dimensions – or from inside the hollow earth.

The noted UFO authority and author, Brinsley le Pour Trench wrote in *Operation Earth* (Neville Spearman, Ltd., 112 Whitfield St., London W1; 1969):

> It is no good trying to evaluate the flying saucers and their occupants on the basis of present knowledge.
>
> The people who ride in flying saucers, whether they are the real Sky People, or those who have their habitat nearer to us, have certain abilities that most of us are not capable of using at the present time.
>
> So, then, that is this 'way-out' extension to the theory of flying saucers emanating from an invisible area surrounding the planet . . . It is that the centre of the earth is hollow and that to some extent the planet is shaped like a doughnut with vast openings at the polar regions, and that an underground race lives in the interior.

Mr. Trench listed some of the books and pamphlets that have been published to support the hollow earth theory. He felt the hypothesis was not entirely acceptable. 'However, we are dealing with a fantastic subject (UFOs) and nothing is impossible,' Mr. Trench admitted. 'Just improbable.'

'. . . . Well, saucers from inside the earth would certainly fit the fantastic,' he concluded.

The Man Who Saw the Smoky God

The old Scandinavian sailor laid back on the wide bed in his cluttered room in a Los Angeles hotel. He was dying and the sour aroma of his illness mingled with the dark odors of human misery in the cheap, skid-row hotel. His only friend was a young, unpublished writer, who sat solemnly in a battered, dirt-covered chair near the death bed.

The old man feebly raised his gray head from a stained pillow. He leaned his weight on a bony arm. A feverish flicker of fear glinted in his eyes.

'Sometimes death takes a long time to reach a man,' he rasped.

'Take it easy, Olaf,' whispered the young writer. 'Your doctor will be here in a few minutes.'

'Forget the doctors. There ain't no cure for old age,' Olaf Jansen said hoarsely. 'But there is still time to tell you about the giants. Maybe you can go there someday.'

'Where's that,' asked Willis George Emerson, the young writer.

'The land beyond the north pole where the giants live,' said the old sailor. 'The world that exists inside the earth.'

As Olaf Jansen waited for death, he told of a strange world inhabited by giants and other supposedly mythical creatures. Jansen stated that he and his father had entered the hollow earth through an opening at the north pole. They had sailed the northern seas in a tiny fishing boat and, when a strong northerly wind drove them northward, they decided to test the tales and myths of their ancestors. Ever since the Scandinavians had sailed out of their fjords in their long warships and fishing vessels, seamen had talked seriously about 'that land beyond the north wind.'

Olaf Jansen claimed that he and his father had sailed into this bizarre world. 'The giants were friendly and we lived there for two years,' he related. 'There were many marvelous wonders inside the earth.'

The dying sailor told of how he was dwarfed by his amiable hosts, a race of giants.

'The giants are not just things in fairy tales,' he rasped. 'They live down there. Like it said in the Bible, they live for five or eight hundred years before they die. They taught us their language.'

'What kind of world is it?' asked the incredulous writer.

'They're much more advanced in doing things,' Jansen said. He explained that the people inside the earth possessed a mysterious power that was greater than electricity. This power source enabled them to operate aircraft by drawing fuel from the atmosphere. The giants in the earth's interior were warmed by a single sun, less brilliant than our solar star. 'This interior sun was dim and they called it the Smoky One or the Smoky God,' Jansen said.

'How did you get out?'

'We got homesick after a couple of years,' answered Olaf Jansen. 'Even paradise can be dull if you don't have friends and relatives with you. The giants allowed us to sail toward home. On the return trip, our little boat was dashed about by giant waves on their ocean. Our compass was lost overboard. We didn't know the directions and we couldn't steer by the North Star. We drifted for a long time and then we were pulled into the south opening at the South Pole.'

Back on the surface world, the two sailors steered northward toward their home. Tragedy struck when an iceberg slammed into the fishing boat. Olaf Jansen's father was apparently killed in the accident. The young sailor was tossed from the deck and out into the frigid waters of the ocean. 'The luck of Leif Ericson was with me,' claimed the old sailor. 'I was rescued by a vessel that had just passed us. They returned me to my home in Norway.'

'But, didn't you tell someone of your adventure?' asked the writer. 'The world would be excited over such a discovery.'

'That was my biggest mistake in life. I did tell them,' replied the old man in a low, bitter tone. 'I started talking about the inner land on the ship. They thought I was crazy. I kept telling them I was not making up stories. When the ship docked in Norway, I was taken off and placed in a mental hospital for the insane. I spent the next twenty-four years of my life in a lunatic's ward!'

Jansen claimed that he entered the asylum as a strong, spirited youth. He left as an embittered, broken, middle-aged man.

'I have a manuscript of my adventures,' he said. 'When I

was in the inner land, I drew some maps of the place. I kept them with me during those twenty-four years in the mental hospital. When I got out, I swore to never show them to anyone again or tell about that place. I wanted to stay free. The way to do that was to keep my mouth shut.'

After his release from the asylum, Olaf Jansen worked as a seaman on fishing boats and saved his pay. He emigrated to the United States, settled for a few years in a small town in Illinois, and eventually moved to California.

'I came to California because it is the one place on earth that looks like the paradise inside the earth,' the dying man claimed.

Before his death, the old sailor provided further details concerning his adventures in the land of the giants. As Willis George Emerson, the writer, had befriended the elderly man, he was heir to the manuscript and maps. Emerson published his original edition of *The Smoky God* in 1908. The book was reprinted in 1965 by Palmer Publications, Amherst, Wisconsin.

We will never know if this strange deathbed story is true or false. The approach of death is a solemn moment for all men, yet a madness to confess seizes the minds of many dying people. They have a compulsion to blurt out their sins and secrets, to cleanse their soul before meeting our Creator. Olaf Jansen's unusual story is bizarre and seemingly fantastic. It is totally unsupported by factual documentation. Maps and manuscripts can also be created out of a writer's imagination, yet Willis George Emerson always maintained that Olaf Jansen was a real man, not a figure conjured up from his writer's mind. Those who believe in the hollow earth, feel that a dying man would not spend his last moments of life in spinning imaginative lies.

The Edge of the World

'Olaf Jansen is just one of the sailors who accidentally journeyed to that land beyond the polar openings,' said

Albert McDonald, the English occultist and president of the Hollow Earth Society. 'Throughout history, mariners have returned home with their astonishing tales of other worlds. They told of strange lands, disappearing islands, sea serpents, uncharted land masses, and unexplained ocean phenomenon.

'The ancients knew the earth was hollow,' McDonald continued. 'They realized that an unwary ship's captain could sail his vessel over the polar rim and down into the inner earth. We feel this is the fact behind the legend of early ships sailing off the edge of the world. This was a danger feared by all ancient seamen, slipping off the edge of the world and down into the unknown void, the inner earth.'

The Hollow Earth Society believes that the legends and myths handed down from ancient times often contain important clues about the interior lands, their inhabitants, plants, and animal life. 'The ancients knew there were these underground kingdoms,' McDonald explained. 'They believed the sailors who returned with stories of subterranean paradises, monster-men, dragons, giants, elves, fairies and unicorns. They listened seriously to accounts of God-like beings, fabled cities of gold, subterranean tunnel cities, and strange animals unknown to the surface world. We've labeled these stories as folklore, dismissing the truths contained within them. Folklore is really the invisible history of mankind.'

Gravity, Holes at the Poles, and Polar Lights

Hollow earth enthusiasts believe the earth is shaped like a doughnut, with openings at the north and south poles. These polar openings lead down onto the land inside the earth. An explorer near the poles might unknowingly pass over these rims. 'There are magnetic aberrations in the compass as you approach the poles,' explained Albert McDonald. 'If you study the history of polar exploration, you find that some explorers lost their bearings. They came back with stories of unusual animals, lush plants, and mosquitos where there should be none. One solution is that these men had gone a way into the hollow earth, or else they found things washed up from the interior worlds.'

Hollow earth believers claim the Arctic and Antarctic oceans flow into the interior of the hollow earth, merging with oceans on the inside. 'Sea serpents, strange marine life, and similar unexplained phenomena have been reported by people who visited these inner oceans,' continued the Englishman. 'From time to time, a sea serpent may swim out into the surface oceans. The beast is sighted by a passing ship and, once again, science claims such animals do not exist and the sighting is dismissed.'

'Gravity is another of those puzzling planetary phenomena,' reported McDonald. 'We're told that gravity is linked to a solid core earth. Yet, few people really know exactly what gravity really is, even in today's highly advanced scientific age. The United States government has embarked on a crash program to understand, and possibly harness, the gravitational power.'

The tall, thin Englishman cupped his slender hands into a circle. 'We don't believe gravity is located at the center of the earth,' he said. 'Look at my hands. Gravity is centered in the shell, or rim, of our planet. A gravitational force holds us in place on the outer surface. In turn, this same gravitational force holds the interior land in place.'

Albert McDonald also has another easy explanation for the polar lights, *Aurora Borealis* and *Aurora Australis*. 'Science has never come forth with a satisfactory explanation for the northern and southern polar lights,' he declared. 'They say these magnificent sky lights are possibly caused by electrical or magnetic storms at the poles. My companions and I feel the *Borealis* and *Australis* are a reflection from the sun in the interior of the earth. "The Smoky God" as Olaf Jansen called it. Light from the inner sun is emitted through the polar openings. It bounces off the earth's atmosphere and is reflected back down on the icy glare of the polar regions and we have these unusual lights.'

Nero's Search for African Treasure Caverns

During his mad reign as Emperor of Rome, Nero depleted the state treasury with some of the most depraved projects in history. He commissioned sculptors to build huge statues of himself, cast in solid gold or carved from enormous blocks of precious stone. About A.D. 60, Nero employed several thousand workmen to construct a small ocean in the palace party room. When the enormous tank was filled with water, he launched a fleet of ships. The Emperor's guests were amused each evening with life-or-death sea battles between opposing fleets manned by terrified slaves.

Such regal behavior disturbed the Roman citizenry and ugly mobs stormed through the streets demanding Nero's head. The Mad Emperor was unperturbed by the angry demonstrations. 'Start a state-sponsored circus,' he informed his aides. 'I want an endless round of gladiators fighting to the death in the arenas. Pit man against man and the victor can be matched against a wild beast. Slake the people's lust for blood in the coliseums!'

In time, the Roman empire was almost bankrupt by such lavish spending. Nero called his financial advisers to the palace for a conference. 'Where can we obtain new funds?' he demanded.

The dour-faced financiers suggested an expedition to the hills of North Africa. 'There are stories of an enormous cavern in the lands of Nubia,' they reported. 'Tunnels run for many miles under the mountains. There are endless rooms piled high with treasure.'

'What sort of treasure?' demanded the emperor.

'Gold, jewels, precious metals, and enormous caskets crammed with rare jewels.'

'Does any man know the entrance to the tunnels?' Nero asked.

'Travelers from those countries say the doorway to these riches have been hidden.'

'Then launch an expedition of legionnaires to seek these riches,' Nero said. 'The empire needs more funds for my projects. The mobs must be appeased with contests and games.'

A detachment of Roman Legionnaires was outfitted and shipped to North Africa. 'You are to find the treasure caverns and ship the valuables back to Rome,' Nero commanded.

Until his death by suicide in A.D. 68, Nero financed the unsuccessful search for the legendary treasure tunnels. The soldiers vainly pursued endless stories about an entrance to the elusive tunnels. If they were camped by the sea, then the entrance was said to be in the mountains. In the fiery African desert, sly Arabs said the tunnel entrance was located in the cities. 'Wherever they went, the tunnel entrance was always located in some other place,' related Albert McDonald, who has gathered research on the expedition. 'Frustrated, yet believing in the underground treasure caverns, the empty-handed Legionnaires were eventually recalled to Rome by Nero's successor.'

Fables of hidden treasure in Africa have intrigued many generations of excited men. 'There are the legendary mines of old King Solomon,' continued Albert McDonald. 'Did they exist? Or, was he simply bringing treasure out of the tunnels? The riches of King Solomon's mines was supposed to have been beyond comprehension, yet no traces remain of where the rare metals were scooped from the earth. Another legend about Aladdin claims he entered a treasure cave with an African magician. Could Aladdin have been a living person who actually entered and returned, from these subterranean vaults?'

Secret Tunnels of the Pyramids

For centuries, occultists have maintained that the Egyptian pyramids contain many elusive secrets. Stories of hidden, undiscovered subterranean vaults and tunnels under the pyramids have been ridiculed by Egyptologists. 'There is supposed to be a connection between the pyramids and the statue of the Great Sphinx through a secret tunnel,' explained Albert McDonald, president of the Hollow Earth Society. 'These underground passages lead to vast chambers beneath these structures where the ancients held their most secret rites.'

Is this wishful thinking by a hollow earth believer? A Roman historian, Ammianus Marcelinus, made these same claims during the hey-day of the Roman empire. Based on reports of Romans who had traveled to Egypt, Marcelinus said the ancient Egyptians forecast the Nile floods, predicted eclipses of the sun, and observed the heavens with instruments hidden under the pyramids.

The Photodrama of the Creation in Word and Picture was published in New York in 1913 with illustrations of the Great Sphinx. A cutaway drawing of that statue revealed five secret chambers and six tunnels that led to an underground area under the pyramids.

'There were two rooms in the head, according to that picture,' explained Albert McDonald. 'A large, massive hall is located in the body and under this is a shaft leading down into an underground pyramid. Another tunnel is constructed still lower, leading down into the heart of the Giza plateau.'

Robert Wilson, who wrote *The History of the British Expedition to Egypt* in 1803 believed there was no entrance into the Sphinx through the head. Since then, Egyptologists have declared that 'the neck of the Sphinx is solid.' During my visit to Egypt, I found that the great Sphinx's head is hollowed out. There is always the possibility that the solid matter in the neck of the gigantic statue is a plug to conceal the entrance to the interior rooms.

These claims of secret shafts, hidden tunnels, and underground vaults should be easily disproven by modern technology and our highly-trained scientists. Yet, there is an elusive, mysterious quality about the pyramids that defies rational explanations. Many scientists condemn occultists for their theories and beliefs about the pyramids. 'I thought the mystery would be solved forever when they planned to X-ray the pyramids with a computerized record of cosmic rays reaching the interior of the structures,' said Albert McDonald.

The six-million-ton mass of stone was to be X-rayed on magnetic tape. The theory was that cosmic rays strike the structure in a uniform pattern from all directions and, therefore, if the pyramid is solid, the rays should be recorded uniformly in the bottom chamber. If there were secret chambers or vaults, more rays would hit the bottom in those areas and reveal the existence of these hidden rooms.

Armed with a new IBM 1130 computer, the scientists quickly discovered that natural laws, as they knew them, did not apply to the pyramids. 'It defies all the known laws of science and electronics,' Dr. Amr Gohed told reporters for the *London Times*, in 1969. He explained that the cosmic ray recordings developed patterns that were completely different from day to day.

'This is scientifically impossible,' Dr. Gohed revealed.

'Has our scientific know-how been rendered useless?' inquired the reporter. 'Is there some force beyond man's comprehension?'

Dr. Gohed hesitated a moment before he replied to the newsmen. 'Either the geometry of the pyramid is in substantial error, which would affect our readings, or there is a mystery which is beyond explanation,' he said. 'Call it what you will, occultism, the curse of the pharaohs, sorcery, or magic – there is some force that defies the laws of science at work in the pyramids.'

Albert McDonald and his followers believe that enigmatic force is powered by the inhabitants of the subterranean lands. 'All of man's history has been written down and deposited in vaults beneath the pyramids,' McDonald declared. 'It will remain there in secrecy until the Masters deem us worthy of handling this vast amount of advanced knowledge.'

Until scientists come up with an accurate report on the pyramids, it appears that pyramidology will continue to be a wild, free-wheeling subject for cultists, theorists, and believers in a hollow earth.

The Secret Subterranean Metropolis

In an article 'About Caves and Other Secret Hiding Places in the World' in the January, 1967, issue of *Search* magazine, author George Wagner Jr. discussed the caverns, caves and tunnels in America. He also published an intriguing report of a vast, subterranean metropolis on the west coast. His account read:

'. . . it brings to mind something written to me recently by one of my correspondents . . . He stated that about 75 miles northwest of Portland, Oregon, between Portland and the Seattle earth-faults, far down in the earth, where the earth once flooded over, is the remains of a splendid city. More recently, Azerland (his informant's name) told me that the city was eight or ten miles (repeat: miles) underground, a coastal city with a fine harbor. It boasted more than a million inhabitants and had an excellent space port.'

If that isn't enough to send a few curious adventurers into the wilds of Washington, then humanity has lost its love of mysteries. I attempted to contact Mr. Wagner for further verification of these statements, but I've been unable to do so. Is the report, fact, fiction, or the imaginative dreams of a Mr. Azerland?

Things In Caves And Tunnels

'I turned around and it looked to be about seven feet tall,' is the way construction laborer Lou Chalmers described his encounter with a 'thing.' Chalmers was a member of a crew of tough Irish laborers who had been hired to construct a tunnel under the Thames river in London in 1969. Almost immediately, the construction crewmen were spooked by a 'thing' that haunted the construction project.

Chalmers was working alone in the tunnel muck when something – or someone – brushed against the back of his neck.

'I figured it was one of the boys,' he told newsmen for the Associated Press. 'I was alarmed to see something with the shape of a man. Its arms were stretched out as if it was trying to get out of something – or grab someone! I didn't stick around to make out the details. I just ran!'

Another worker, George (Nobby) O'Brien, came dashing out of the tunnel one day.

'He was white as a sheet,' said Colin Cobb, another laborer. 'He told me he had seen the figure of a man or something like a man down there. He went for a big, stiff drink. He quit his job and we haven't seen him since.'

Whatever O'Brien saw in the tunnel must have been a frightening spectre. He was earning $312 a week when he walked away from the job.

Irishmen have always talked about subterranean people, wee folk, fairies, and elves. 'It isn't anything like that,' reported Tom McGee to a researcher from the Hollow Earth Society. 'This thing wears a brown overcoat and a cap. Some of the boys say it isn't an overcoat, but a robe of some kind. Maybe it's the ghost of somebody who was buried down there when London was struck by the black plague a few centuries ago.'

Another English laborer was digging underground in 1770 and may have obtained a brief glimpse of the technology of an inner earth culture. In Vol. 1, No. 6 of the *Newsletter for the Committee for the Scientific Evaluation of Psi*, author and researcher Ronald Calais said the tunnel worker was digging in the earth when he was attracted by a strange noise behind a huge, smooth-surfaced stone.

The laborer was intrigued and he prised away the stone. He gazed incredulously at a stone stairway that winded down into the earth. Cautiously, and possibly intrigued with thoughts of ancient tombs and buried treasure, the workman walked down the stairway. A few moments later, the puzzled man entered an enormous stone cavity in the earth. The cavern contained smooth walls and a level stone floor – and several enormous machines. The room was illuminated by a light.

The astonished laborer started to inspect the room when a robed, hooded figure dashed toward him, running frantically down a long aisle. The strangely-clad subterranean being had an angry look on his face and he held a metallic wand in his hand. Terrified by the unusual creature, the frightened laborer dashed back up the stairway. Breathless and gasping for air in the tunnel, he slammed the flat stone back over the entrance to the weird cavern.

'There is nothing more known about that old account,' admitted Albert McDonald. 'Possibly the laborer was so frightened that he simply kept his mouth shut until he was safely away from the tunnel. For whatever reason, the tunnel workers around Staffordshire were not eager to explore that cavern.'

Could it be possible that a slender thread of reality exists in these myths, legends, stories, and factual accounts of unexplained phenomena? Could there be a civilization in the interior of the earth, an ageless land that has remained hidden from surface humanity? Could the 'hollow earth' actually be a world in another dimension that co-exists beside our own? The discovery of such a world could be one of the most important discoveries in the history of our planet. Or, it could lead to one of the most horrible eras of human history.

MYSTERY OF THE HOLE IN THE POLES

Ray Palmer, editor and publisher of *Flying Saucer* magazine and several occult publications, has been one of the most prominent personalities on the UFO scene during the past two decades. Once, the U.S. Air Force accused Palmer of triggering the whole UFO mystery as a publicity hoax to sell magazines. Ray Palmer has long been an articulate champion for civilian flying saucer research. His habit of championing numerous unorthodox, occult theories has made both the occult and scientific Establishments anxious to reinstate burning at the stake as punishment for heretical views.

It frequently comes as a surprise to discover that the 'father of flying saucers' does not believe in the popular conception of flying saucers. 'It's true,' Palmer told Brad Steiger and Warren Smith during an interview for *Saga* magazine. 'I don't believe in flying saucers – at least not in the popular concept of flying saucers that John Q. Public interprets as being synonymous with alien spacecraft from outer space.

'I *do* believe in whatever reality is behind the flying saucer mystery,' Palmer explained. 'But, this reality is at the present time unknown.'

Ray Palmer was the controversial editor of the popular Ziff-Davis pulp magazines for many years. In the 1940s, he left the big city and returned to his native Wisconsin. Today, Palmer lives on a farm near Amherst, Wisconsin, a few miles from the converted school building that houses his Amherst Press. Palmer is editor and publisher of *Flying Saucers, Search, Space World, Rocket Exchange,* and the *Forum*. When he is not busy editing his magazines, Palmer wanders about his 124-acre woodland farm. In rare moments away from his editing and publishing chores, Palmer likes to cast for fish in the trout streams and private lake on his farm.

'The first thing a "true believer" says when he meets me,' Palmer grinned, 'is "Aha! You really are a man from Mars!"'

Ray Palmer is a diminutive man, standing only four feet eight inches in height. This small stature is due to a crippling childhood disease and not to any unusual environmental conditions on Mars or some other planet. While he is physically small, Ray Palmer has cast a giant shadow over UFOs and occultism. Frequently, his published reports have angered government agencies, the scientific establishment, and the entrenched members of the occult establishment.

Palmer outlined his philosophy during the interview:

> You want to know why I think the Air Force and the government have been suppressing knowledge about UFOs? Let me draw just a quick parallel with the LSD problem.
>
> Now we have only the government's word that LSD is bad, that it must be suppressed, and whenever the government tells me that I must not have something, I begin to wonder why that is.
>
> Please understand that I have never taken LSD and have no interest in doing so, but several proponents of LSD have told me that they see not an illusion, but a reality beyond the ordinary. These people believe their mystical experiences under the influences of LSD are genuine and profoundly meaningful.
>
> The one inescapable fact of history is that the people who are in control want to stay in control. There's always the guy who wants to rule. He wants nothing to upset the *status quo*.
>
> UFO, ESP, LSD, the 'hippies' – these things could force the scientists, the clergy, the AMA, and the educators to revise most of their cherished concepts of what makes the universe tick.
>
> I believe that there is a basic reality behind the UFOs

and paranormal phenomena. I believe these things have a common place of origin – an area not commonly connected with the five senses – perhaps something within each of us. Perhaps those who harnessed this power in the past became 'masters' who could control time, space, and physical matter. When it comes right down to it, we really don't know much about ourselves. But people sense that these things really do exist.

If this is so, there is little wonder why the Establishment feels compelled to ridicule and stop serious research in these areas.

Although Ray Palmer keeps an open mind to all elements of the UFO mystery, he is convinced the answer to the phenomena is on our own planet and not in outer space. 'The more you consider the extra-terrestrial thesis, the more impossible it becomes to prove,' Ray Palmer stated. 'UFOs have been seen in the skies since man's prehistory, and today there seems to be a virtual traffic jam of objects coming in from somewhere. It seems, to me, difficult to conceive that ours should be the only planet of any interest to extraterrestrial life forms.

'. . . The supposition that the saucers have an earth base and may be manned by an older terrestrial race brings the cosmic concept down to reality,' Palmer continued. 'Geographically speaking, our own atmosphere is a heck of a lot closer than Alpha Centauri!'

Ray Palmer does not discount the possible reality of underground cities. 'I do not deny the possible existence of these underground cultures,' he said. 'One can find reference to them in the most primitive oral traditions and right up to our contemporary accounts.' He also believes that some of these underground civilizations may be in existence today.

Over the years, Palmer has explored the theory of a hollow earth in his magazines. One of his most controversial issues was the June, 1970, issue of *Flying Saucers* magazine. Palmer published an editorial on several photographs he had obtained. The photographs were obtained from U.S. Government agencies and they were taken by our ESSA satellites. Palmer's editorial brewed up a roaring controversy that has not yet subsided. It reads:

> On our cover this month we reproduce the most remarkable photograph ever made. It was taken by ESSA-7 satellite on November 23, 1968. On the opposite page we reproduce another picture taken the same day by the same satellite with the same camera under the same conditions. Both are official, unretouched photos provided by the Environmental Science Service Administration, U.S. Department of Commerce. The grid patterns of latitudes was printed automatically by computer calculations when the picture was taken, and therefore are an integral part of the original photograph for purposes of exact identification of the areas shown in the photos.
>
> The photo on the front cover is of the north pole. Both show the remarkable clear photograph of the cloud cover on that day over both poles. Both depict about 40 per cent of the Earth's total area. As of December 10, 1969, ESSA-7 had taken 39,953 pictures, when it was placed on standby mode. During 481 days, the cover photo is the only one which shows a total lack of cloud cover . . .
>
> The north pole photo, lacking clouds in the polar area, therefore reveals the surface of the planet. Although surrounding the polar area, and north of such areas as the North American continent and Greenland, and the Asian continent, we can see the ice fields of the 8-foot thick ice . . . (in the photo) we do not see any ice fields in a large circular area directly at the geographic pole. Instead, we see—
>
> THE HOLE!

We might pause for a moment in Palmer's editorial and report that the photograph taken by the satellite was reproduced without retouching in the magazine. Directly in the center of the photograph was a small, circular dark area.

To the casual observer, this would certainly support Palmer's conception that the earth is hollow and one entrance into the inner lands is an opening at the polar areas. Palmer continues:

> One of the severest criticisms leveled at us during past years because of our theorizing concerning a hole at the pole and a hollow Earth has been the fact that none of the photos (well over a million and a half of them) taken from satellites have shown such a hole. There have been a half-dozen taken from orbits which have shown the dark area visible in this photo, but (they) were impossible to record as definite photographic resolution of such a phenomena as a hole.
>
> NOW WE HAVE A PHOTO!
>
> However, in order to bolster our own position even further, if that would be *necessary* (!), we want to forestall the point that is sure to be made that it is unwise to base a conclusion on a single photo. It could be a defect! So, we present two photos of the same area, the north and south poles, taken by ESSA-3 on January 6, 1967. Once again a fortunate and rare circumstance of lack of cloud cover over the north pole reveals—
>
> THE HOLE!
>
> If flying saucers have been in the top secret file, then the place they might come from would certainly be (secret)! Passing over the subject of flying saucers, there are many more reasons why a hole at the pole would be classified information. Militarily, it would be highly significant, particularly if the inside of the earth is inhabited (perhaps by a race far superior to us, scientifically and technologically).

More modern concepts of the formation of planets adopt the 'vortex' or 'whirlpool' theory, which states that bodies in space are formed by rotating motion in the ether which collects matter at its center, gradually adding to it until it becomes a sun or a planet or a satellite or a comet

– and that is the process, the semi-spherical object has the typical formation of a vortex, such as you observe in the water going down the bathtub drain, of a 'hole at the center of a swirl'. Thus, in this theory quite widely held by astronomers and physicists, many planetary bodies still have this hole at the center of the whirl that has formed them.'

Palmer explained that when astronomers look through their telescopes, they are able to view the spiral nebulae in space and each of these space objects have a hole in the center. Recent photographs taken of Mars revealed a circular, unusually dark circle at the planet's geographic poles. To date, science is unable to determine if the Martian polar caps are composed of some unusual substance. There are also ancient astronomers' reports that while they observed the planet Mercury passing the sun, during a Mercurial eclipse, a tiny, bright dot was observed on the planet. Several astronomers have categorized the glowing dot as simply an illusion; others have reported it was simply an accident. Palmer says: '. . . today we can wonder if it isn't true that just at that moment, the polar orifice of Mercury, formed as other bodies by a vortexial action, had not presented itself at precisely the proper position to be observed?'

The scientific establishment merely shakes its collective head, shrugs its shoulders in an amused gesture, and says such theories are not worthy of investigation. 'Anyone can carefully select facts and build up a circumstantial case for any theory,' an astro-physicist informed me. 'The north and south poles have both been discovered. There are simply no unexplored land masses in this planet. Airlines fly their jets over the north pole every day.'

In his editorial, however, Ray Palmer pointed out that 'over-the-pole' flights were a myth. '. . . we have answered critics who claim that the airlines fly over the pole daily, by publishing an admission of the airline that this is poetic license,' Palmer wrote. '. . . actually they do not come within

150 miles of the geographic pole because of the non-functioning of navigational instruments.'

Palmer concluded his editorial with these words:

> All we can say is that you have asked why no pictures taken from space show the hole at the pole. Our answer to that is that such pictures are rare, because of constant cloud cover, and the difficulty of identifying the planet from space. Our satellites even say the earth is uninhabited! And of course, our answer is – there are the pictures, and here *are* two two of them!
>
> Even in Biblical days, the existence of this cloud cover was known, and its effectiveness in hiding the secret was well known. Let me quote a few: (All of these are from the book of Job.)
>
> 'He stretcheth out the north over the empty place . . .'
>
> 'He bindeth up the waters in his thick clouds; and the cloud is not rent under them.'
>
> 'By the breath of God, frost is given; and the breadth of the waters is straightened.'
>
> 'Hast thou entered into the treasures of the snow? Or hast thou seen the treasures of the hail? Which I have reserved against the time of trouble, against the day of battle and war.'
>
> 'Out of whose womb came the ice? And the hoary frost of heaven, who hath engendered it?'
>
> 'The waters are hid as with a stone, and the face of the deep is frozen.'
>
> The following quotations are from Isaiah:
>
> 'For thou has said in thine heart, I will ascend into heaven, I will exalt my throne above the stars of God; I will sit upon the stars of God; I will sit upon the mount of the congregation, in the sides of the north.'
>
> 'Yet thou shalt be brought down to hell, to the sides of the pit.'
>
> Ephesians says:

'Now that he is ascended, what is it but that he also descended first into the lower parts of the earth?'

In Psalms, we find:

'He made darkness his secret place; his pavillion round about him were dark waters and thick clouds in the skies.'

'Then the channels of the waters were seen, and the foundations of the world were discovered at thy rebuke. O Lord, at the blast of the breath of thy nostrils. He brought me forth into a large place; he delivered me because he delighted in me.'

Generally, in the Bible, reference is made to a 'pit,' variously called Sheol, Abbadon, Appolyon, the deeps, the sides of the north, the foundation of the earth, and that a throne of God exists 'in the sides of the pit,' or in Abbadon, etc. And it is hidden beneath the clouds, and made inaccessible by ice.

It would seem that the Bible, in its weird references to the frozen north, to the pit there, how it is perpetually hidden by clouds and guarded by ice, might also be recording accurately.

Job said: 'He stretcheth out the north over the empty place...'

Admiral Byrd said: 'That enchanted continent in the sky, that land of everlasting mystery!'

Admiral Byrd, in his polar expeditions, stood 'in the sides of the north' and, looking up, could see the other side hanging mysteriously in the sky, probably 800 miles (more or less) away. Perhaps Job saw that same mysterious land of the north, 'stretched out over the empty place' in the 'treasures of the snow.'

ESSA-7 and ESSA-3 have produced photos which render it entirely credible – RAP.

Palmer's astonishing editorial and the published photographs quickly became the subject of a swirling controversy in the occult world. Many 'believers' were firmly convinced that Ray Palmer had finally obtained conclusive evidence to prove the 'hole-at-the-pole.' Some non-believers adopted an open-minded attitude and waited for more data and information. Still others expressed the opinion that Ray Palmer was attempting to create a hoax. Regardless of their opinions, many people were visibly shaken by Palmer's material in that June, 1970, edition of *Flying Saucers* magazine.

A number of readers wrote directly to Palmer at his office in Amherst, Wisconsin. In his *Flying Saucers* edition of September, 1970, Palmer printed several of these letters and replied to his critics. One reader wrote:

> Dear Ray:
>
> 'I'm shook by your statement in the June '70 editorial of *Flying Saucers* magazine, that the ESSA-7 photo (11-23-68) shows 'we do not see any ice fields in a large circular area directly at the geographic pole. Instead, we see – The Hole!'
>
> *You've been had!* . . . the large hole which most readers must assume you are referring to, extends down to the middle of Greenland, and includes Baffin Island, and Ellesmereland Island, not to mention Novaya Zemla (and the ordinary Arctic ocean) is included in that big hole in the cloud cover.
>
> Just compare the photo and latitude marks (placed by the computer in the photo as you say) with a North Pole region map in your atlas. The latitude circle just inside the 'hole' is 70 degrees north. Incidentally, the photo is a composite paste-up, placed over a sphere for rephotographing. Look at the seam running about 2 o'clock. (So, it was a clear day over the pole. So what? No hole shows).

Ray Palmer replied by stating the reader was 'shook, but not shook enough.' He added:

> You are not shook enough to check your own state-

ments. If you are going to be in the business of debunking Ray Palmer, you will have to quit making 'suppositions' and avoid any rationalization. First, I did not say that the entire blank area was the hole (if it really is a hole). It is my opinion that the hole has to be not more than 800 miles in diameter, and probably less. Yes, the computers placed the overlay of Greenland inside the dark area. It had to, because the computer is programmed to conceive of the planet as a perfect sphere without a hole, and it is programmed to include all of Greenland even when the camera does not delineate the total area of the overlay. But where you go into the realm of supposition, is the method used to take the photo presented. It is a composite (either 3 or 6 exposures, because the camera is capable of such latitude on each pass over the pole, at the discretion of ground control). But it is not a composite paste-up placed over a sphere and rephotographed. It is a 3-or-6 radio-received photos pasted together and then reproduced as you see it in the magazine. – Ray Palmer.

Another reader discussed the daylight at the poles. 'I don't think the cover photo on your June, 1970, issue shows the hole at the pole . . .' he wrote, and concluded, '. . . In my opinion, if there is a hole in the polar regions, it is in the head of the propounder of the idea.' The writer of the letter, a radioscope operator in the Arctic region, reported that the various government scientific specialists had been throughout the Arctic without 'seeing any evidence of the hole.'

'Now, recently, the most fascinating discovery of the polar area of all has been made with the revelation that as we approach the pole,' Palmer replied, 'the surface of the ocean *begins* to slant toward the north . . . Every high school student knows that the absolutely infallible way to find a level and construct something on that level is to use the surface of water, which *never* tilts. Now why, 800 miles from the pole, does the water suddenly begin to tilt in that direction? Obviously gravity has something to do with it. Either gravity is no longer functioning directly toward the center of the earth, or the center of the mass is being dislocated (by the fact of an increasing angle of descent into a depression, the surface of which is at right angles to this displacement of the center of gravity of the Earth's mass.)'

Palmer explored the mysterious phenomena that polar explorers have reported. '. . . . Lots of little things like the distance to the east-west horizon, which so baffled Nansen, being greater than the distance to the north-south horizon at this same 800 mile location, were part of the mystery,' Palmer said. 'It would take a very thick book to present all the strange facts that are not explainable without postulating some such thing as a hole at the pole, a hollow earth, or something. Maybe it's only a depressed area, and not a hole all of the way through, or into the center. But whatever it is, it is something, and one thing is sure, it is *not* the billard ball smoothness over its entire surface that the world is supposed to be!'

As the controversy continued, Ray Palmer added many fascinating items to the lore of the hollow earth mystery. They include:

Admiral Byrd's Polar Flights: '. . . I live in Amherst, Wisconsin. It is three miles from Nelsonville. Nelsonville was the home of Lloyd K. Grenlie. He more recently lived in Green Bay, where he served in the Federal Aviation Agency for many years before he died June 7, 1970. His family are my neighbors. This is important only because Lloyd K. Grenlie was the radioman on Admiral Byrd's expedition to the south pole in 1926 and to both poles in 1929. In 1929 a newsreel could be seen in America's theaters which described *both* flights, and also showed newsreel photos of the 'land beyond the pole (north) with its mountains, trees, rivers and a large animal identified as a mammoth.'

'Today, this newsreel does not exist, although hundreds of my readers remember, as I do, seeing this movie short. Thus, I have it on my own personal viewing . . . and from the radioman who went with Byrd to that land beyond the pole and *saw* the things recorded on film, that this unknown, uncharted, and presently denied land exists!'

Polar Gravity: '. . . The only reason there are polar orbiting satellites today is because the launchers took into consideration the anomalies of gravity directly over the pole. Prior to that, we lost every satellite launched on a precise polar orbit. The Russians have hinted (strongly!) that the only logical place to establish easy space travel off this Earth is at the poles. And they hint equally strongly the reason why – gravity. It is weird to understand that scientists as able as they are would even suggest that gravity might not be a factor inhibiting rocket launches from that point, and even more weird, the suggestion that there might be planets without gravity, where no retro-rockets are needed to land!'

Cloud Photography: '. . . . How about somebody actually in the cloud-photographing business, including the polar satellites, sending me a print of those photos which in his opinion will shatter my theory to bits? It would be impossible for me to go through hundreds of thousands of photos looking for some 'clinchers', even if they would be sent to me! Or, is it true that there is secrecy and censorship? My point is this: if there is no hole, it would be to the public good to show up such goofs as me, with some facts. But if there is a hole – and you know it – I challenge your right to keep it a secret from me! In my mind, science cannot be political. If it kowtows to the politician or to the military, it is worthy of all the epithets and curses that can be heaped upon its collective head. Any scientist who is not true to his fellow man in passing on his discoveries for the betterment of all and of all knowledge is a scoundrel!

'. . . Yes! I had a very good reason for presenting these photographs – very good ones! There is not a person in this world who has ever read any of my magazines who can say that I have ever fooled or tricked him! All of them will agree that many of the things I have presented have later fallen flat on their faces, but not because I lied about them!

... I gave you a chance to see for yourself, decide for yourself, refute or support me if you could!'

The North Pole – From the Russian View: In the March, 1962, issue of *Flying Saucers* magazine, Ray Palmer described the intriguing discoveries of Russian polar explorers. He felt that many of these discoveries strengthened the concept of a hollow earth with openings at the north and south polar regions. The article was subtitled as 'More Evidence of Mystery Lands at the Poles – Two Hundred Years of Exploration Have Given the Russians a New Concept of the Pole and Render All Previous Geographies Obsolete; Here Are Indisputable Geophysical Facts.' A selection from this article follows:

> There is something mysterious about each polar area of the Earth. We have suggested that there is much more 'area' at both poles than it is possible to show on a globe map. We have pointed out Admiral Byrd's strange flights 'beyond' the poles. We have mentioned the case of missing mountains and different branches of the military discounting the mapping ability of the other. We have even suggested that the earth is hollow, and that giant ... openings exist at the poles, and there is much evidence of the existence of these openings. We have pointed out that there is a great deal of secrecy and double-talk about the Arctic and Antarctic areas. We have even suggested that flying saucers might come from this mystery area, or from inside the earth.
>
> One of the things we have been most insistent about is that no one has yet been to the North Pole, all claims to having done so being false, because the Pole is not a 'point,' and cannot be 'reached' in the accepted sense of the word.
>
> We have successfully challenged those military and civilian pilots who have claimed that they fly 'daily' over the North Pole. In the case of the military flyer we have pointed out the maneuver which is standard, which auto-

matically makes it impossible for him to fly 'beyond' the Pole by flying straight across it. (That is, across the polar opening, instead of going into it – Author.) Because of 'navigating difficulties stemming from compasses of all kinds' a 'lost' flier (whose compass doesn't work as it should) regains his bearings by making a turn in any direction, until his compasses again resume function. In the case of commercial airlines, whose advertising boast is that they fly twice daily over the Pole, they are simply stretching the truth by 2,300 miles. (They simply cross over the magnetic rim of the polar opening, where the compass registers the highest degree north, but do not actually reach the North Pole, which is the central point of the polar opening inside this rim – Author.)

We have available, in the form of records of several hundred years, in Russian archives, a history of Arctic exploration which proves our most important point beyond further question: i.e., that the North Magnetic Pole is not a point, but (deduce the Russians) a 'line' approximately 1000 miles long. Before we go further, we might suggest that we think they are wrong in this deduction, and that instead of being a line, it is actually a circle. Because of lack of space to place it on the globe, the Russians have been forced to compress their observations into a two dimensional area. They had to squeeze the circle from two sides and make a line out of it. We'd like to give you now a resumé of that single point of Russian exploration, which actually covers much more than just geomagnetism.

Here is what the Russians say: 'Navigators in the high latitudes have always been troubled by the odd behavior of their magnetic compasses caused by apparent irregularities and asymmetries in the magnetic field of the earth. Early magnetic maps have been drawn on this assumption, based on hopeful guesses, that the North Magnetic Pole is virtually a point. Accordingly, it was expected that the compass needle, which dips more steeply as it approaches the Magnetic Pole, would point straight down, or very nearly so, at the Magnetic Pole itself. But data from many Russian and other expeditions showed that the compass needle points straight down for a very long distance across the Arctic Ocean, from a point northwest of the Taimyr Peninsula to another point in the Arctic Archipelago. This discovery first inspired the hypothesis that there is a second North Magnetic Pole, tentatively located at 86 degrees East longitude. More refined observation has disposed of this idea. The map of the magnetic field now shows the magnetic meridians running close together in a thick bunch of lines from the North Magnetic Pole in the Arctic Archipelago to Siberia. *The North Magnetic Pole, once thought to be virtually a point in the Arctic Archipelago, has been shown by recent investigations to extend across the polar basin to the Taimyr Peninsula in Siberia.*

The 'Pole' magnetically speaking, is a very extended area that crosses the Polar Basin from one continent to the other. It is at least 1,000 miles long, and more likely can be said to exist as a rather diffused line for 1,000 miles more. (It is really not a point in the far north, but is the rim of the polar opening, since after Admiral Byrd passed it and entered the polar opening leading to the Earth's interior, he left the Arctic ice and snow behind and entered a warmer territory – Author.) Thus when Admiral Peary (and any other Arctic explorer who used a magnetic compass) claims to have 'reached' the Pole, he is making a very vague claim indeed. He can only say that he reached a point, which can be anywhere in a demonstrable 2,000 mile area (the magnetic rim of the polar opening), where his compass pointed straight down. A noteworthy achievement, but not a 'discovery of the Pole.'

Since other types of compass, such as the gyroscopic and the inertial guidance, have equally vague limitations, we make bold to say that *nobody ever reached* the Pole, and more, there is not a 'pole' to reach.

Next, having found themselves stumped to account for the strange behavior of the compass in the Polar Basin, the theorists have turned to space and the upper atmosphere and even to the sun for an explanation of what is happening to their instruments. Now the Pole has become 'the interaction of the magnetic field with charged particles from the sun.'

More significant are the unfavorable references to former cartographers whose maps are now 'thick clouds congealed in the imagination of cartographers as land masses.' The Navy, as an example, feels a bit put out when the Army says their missing South Pole mountains were never there, because the Army cannot find them by their own confused reckoning based on a magnetic pole which 'isn't there at all.' We find now that new land areas are 'discovered' and old maps tossed out because the lands they show are not there any more. (This confusion is due to the irregular action of the compass in the far north due to the fact that the North Magnetic Pole is not a point as former cartographers supposed, but a circle around the rim of the polar opening – Author.)

This brings us to the subject of 'mystery lands' of great extent in the polar areas, which cannot possibly be placed on our globe without overlapping seriously in impossible ways . . . Could it be here where the flying saucers originate?

It is well known that the North and South Magnetic Poles do not coincide with the geographical poles, as they should were the Earth a solid sphere, convex at its poles. The reason why the magnetic and geographical poles don't coincide is because, while the magnetic pole lies along the rim of the polar opening, the geographical pole lies in its center, in midair and not on solid land. As we shall see below, the true magnetic pole is not on the external rim of the polar opening but the center of the earth's crust, which should be about 400 miles below the surface, and running around the polar opening. For this reason, the needle of the compass still continues to point vertically downward after one passes the rim of the polar opening and penetrates into it. Only after passing its center would the needle of the compass start pointing upward, instead of downward, but in either case, after reaching the rim of the polar opening, the compass no longer functions horizontally, as previously, but vertically. This has been observed by all Arctic explorers who reached high latitudes and (the phenomena) puzzled them. The only explanation is provided on the conception of a hollow earth and polar openings, with the magnetic pole and the center of gravity in the middle of the earth's crust, and not in its geometrical center. As a result, ocean water on the inside of the crust adheres to its inner surface, just as it does on the outside. We may calculate the Earth's magnetic pole and center of gravity as a circular line around the polar opening, but in its middle, about 400 miles from the earth's surface.

'They tell us over and over again that there are no spaceships from Mars,' Ray Palmer said, recently. Fine. I'll accept that. Tell me where UFOs really come from and what they really are. But don't keep telling me that there are *no* such things as unidentified flying objects, that LSD produces *only* hallucinations, that ESP is simply a delusion.'

Is the hollow earth theory fact or fiction? Is it possible that behind this fascinating intellectual exercise is an astonishing truth? 'From now on, the burden of proof is on the other side,' Ray Palmer reported recently. '—to prove that there is no hole at the pole!'

(*Author's note*: Palmer's controversial photographs of the alleged hole at the pole were published in the Journal of the SMPHE, February, 1970 issue. The photographs may possibly be obtained from the Environmental Science Service, U.S. Department of Agriculture, Washington, D.C. Copies of the controversial June, 1970, issue of *Flying Saucers* magazine may possibly be available from Palmer Publications, Inc. Rte. 2, Box 36, Amherst, Wisconsin, 54406.)

According to Buddhist doctrine, Agharta is a subterranean land located deep within the center of our planet. The Buddhists believe there are millions of people living in this underworld paradise. Their daily lives and ultimate destiny are directed by a wise, all-powerful ruler known as Rigden-jyepo – the King of the World, Rigden-jyepo reigns in Shamballah, the capital city of Agharta, one of the most beautiful cities in the universe.

'From his palace in Shamballah, Rigden-jyepo also directs many of the activities of *homo sapiens* on the surface world,' reported Gunther Rosenberg. His European Occult Research Society has conducted widespread research into the legends of the Far East. 'The King of the World is allegedly in close communication with the Dalai Lama, spiritual leader of Tibet. These messages from the underworld are carried by emissaries, a corps of subterranean monks who have been trained as secret couriers from Agharta. They are supposed to travel to and from Agharta through a vast network of underground tunnels. These secret tunnels are supposed to be connected to many of the ancient Tibetan monasteries and, of course, the surface entrance is carefully guarded by monks selected by the Dalai Lama. These Tibetan tunnels are just part of a honeycomb of tunnels linking many parts of the world.'

Nicholas Roerich (1874–1947), was a noted Russian artist, explorer, and philosopher. A talented individual with mystical inclinations, Roerich also had a lengthy association with the Moscow Art Theater and the Diaghilev Ballet Company. In the nineteen twenties, Roerich spent five years exploring the Himalayan mountains, Tibet, and the isolated regions of Asia.

'Roerich's artistic accomplishments almost obscure his scientific achievements,' explained Gunther Rosenberg. 'He is listed in the encyclopedia as an archeologist. Roerich became convinced that Lhasa, the Tibetan capital, was connected to Shamballah by a network of tunnels. He said these same tunnels connected to the Great Pyramid at Giza, where there is a mysterious subterranean chamber. He felt the old pharaohs of Egypt were in contact with the super gods of the underworld, through emissaries from Shamballah.'

Buddhist scripture claims that Agharta was founded many millions of years ago, far back in the dim era of pre-history. 'A great holy man was warned by the gods of an impending disaster,' explained Gunther Rosenberg. 'He led his people down through the tunnels and into the inner lands. This has elements of the Biblical story of Noah, along with a touch of the catastrophe that allegedly destroyed Atlantis.'

Why and when do the representatives of Agharta come to the surface world?

'Buddhist tradition claims these visitations occur during times of great turmoil,' continued Gunther Rosenberg. 'UFOs, or flying saucers, appeared shortly after the nuclear explosions during World War II that heralded man's entrance into the atomic age. Some people believe that man's knowledge of atomic energy is a threat to this entire planet. Hence, they feel these god-like supermen from the hollow earth are maintaining a close watch over surface activities.'

In his out-of-print book, *Shamballah* (Frederick Stokes & Company; New York; 1930) Nicholas Roerich wrote of his experiences in Tibet. In the opening chapter, 'Shamballah, The Resplendent,' the Russian archeologist told of his conversation with a high lama in Tibet in his visit to that land in 1928.

'Lama, tell me of Shamballah,' Roerich said.

'But you Westerners know nothing of Shamballah,' the lama answered. 'You wish to know nothing. Probably you ask out of curiosity; and you pronounce the sacred word in vain.'

'Lama, I don't ask about Shamballah aimlessly,' Roerich replied. 'Everywhere, people know of this great symbol under different names. Our scientists seek each new spark containing this remarkable realm. Csoma de Koros knew of Shamballah, when he made his prolonged visits to the Buddhist monasteries. Grunwendel translated the book of the famous Tashi Lama, pal-den-ye-she, about the "Way to Shamballah." We sense how under these sweet symbols, a great truth is concealed...'

The lama stared intently at Nicholas Roerich for a moment, looking at the Russian scientist with unblinking, piercing eyes. Roerich and the lama were alone in a long room in the monastery. The lama broke the silence of the darkened room by clapping his hands. A monk appeared with tea in two porcelain cups on a gold tray. As they sipped the bitter liquid, the lama explained that Shamballah was simply an enormous celestial kingdom, akin to the heavenly kingdom of the Christian religion.

Roerich was not content with this explanation. He placed a portfolio of notes on a rug between them. 'Lama, I have heard of the reality of this indescribable place – an earthly Shamballah. I've been told that some high lamas have visited Shamballah. I've heard of the Vuryat Lama and how he was taken through a narrow, secret passageway. So, please don't tell me of only the heavenly Shamballah because I know that a real one exists on earth. I and you both know that these earthly and heavenly Shamballah are linked together, with the two worlds unified.'

The lama meditated for several minutes. The only sound in the room was the gentle tinkle of distant prayer bells. 'He is there in Shamballah,' the old Tibetan holy man said. 'Vigilant, indefatigable, and with his magical mirror he can tune in on all the events on this planet. He is Rigden-jyepo and his might is such that distance does not exist for him. He has been known to bring instantaneous aid to those he considers worthy. His riches are there to assist the needy. He is so powerful that he may change the karma of humans.'

After a description of the supernatural power of the King

of the World, the lama added: 'Uncountable are the inhabitants of that marvelous land! There are many new forces and achievements being prepared for those of us on the surface world...'

'Lama, the Vedanta says that very soon a new energy will be given to humanity,' Roerich said.

'There are numerous things being prepared under predestiny,' replied the lama. 'Through our Holy Books we become acquainted with the teachings of the Blessed One. We have heard of this new energy. We have heard about the inhabitants of distant stars. We have also heard of the flying steel birds . . . and of iron serpents that devour space with fire and smoke.'

Roerich informed the lama of an experience when he traveled in the deserts of Asia. 'Lama, a huge black vulture flew close to our camp when we remained near Ulan-Davan,' the Russian said. 'The vulture crossed the direction of something shining and beautiful, which flew over our camp and glistened in the rays of the sun.'

'Did you smell an unusual fragrance at that time?' the lama inquired eagerly.

'We were in a large desert and several days' march away from the nearest settlement,' said Roerich. 'Yet, we became aware of a strange, exquisite perfume. I've never smelt such lovely perfume.'

'You are watched over by Shamballah,' declared the Tibetan. '. . . the protecting forces of Shamballah have guarded you in the Radiant Form of Matter. This force is always close to the Chosen Ones – although, they may not be aware of its existence. On occasion, this force is manifested for directing you. Whatever direction the sphere may have moved, you should follow that same direction. You have also mentioned the sacred calls – *Kalagiva!* When an individual hears this call, he knows that the route to Shamballah is open for him!' The lama informed his Russian visitor that anyone who hears the cry of *Kalagiva* is henceforth given assistance by the Blessed Rigden-jyepo – The

King of the World. 'You must know the way in which help is given,' he advised, 'because people can often repel the help which is given.'

Roerich was also interested in how the secret of Shamballah was guarded. He asked, 'Does Shamballah have many messengers throughout the world? How are the secrets entrusted to them protected?'

'There is a great Keeper of the Mysteries,' explained the lama. 'He watches closely over those who have been given important missions and secret work. If a sudden evil should threaten the couriers, they are given immediate assistance. The entrusted treasure must forever be guarded. Forty years ago, a man who lived in the Mongolian Gobi desert was entrusted with a secret treasure. When he felt he was about to die of old age, he tried to find a worthy soul to give the secret to before death claimed him. He was unable to find anyone in a state of worthiness. But the great Keeper of the Mysteries was ever vigilant and he reached the sick man, revived his spirits, and permitted him to find a purified individual to entrust the treasure.'

'Why didn't the Keeper of the Mysteries take the treasure with him?'

The lama sighed and closed his eyes for a moment. 'Karma has its special ways and even the renowned Keeper of the Mysteries does not wish to touch the threads of Karma. A single Karmic thread that is broken can result in tremendous harm and danger.'

Roerich told of his travels in Tourfan and Turkestan, where he was shown long caves with secret passages and long, unexplored tunnels. 'Can a person follow these caves to reach the Ashrams of Shamballah?' he inquired. 'We were informed that on occasion people – strangers to those regions – came out of those caves. These strange beings went into the cities and purchased supplies with ancient, strange coins of an unknown mintage.'

'Verily, verily,' chanted the lama. 'People from Shamballah do sometimes visit into the surface world. These visits are to meet with the earthly co-workers of the powerful Rigden-jyepo. They may also visit to send forth remarkable gifts and precious relics. Even Rigden-jyepo has been known to appear in human form in the monasteries. These visits are predestined and he makes his prophecies for the future.'

The lama related that when the King of the World appears before surface man, his visit heralds the approach of a great epoch in human events. 'Many events are now being manifested,' the Tibetan continued. 'The cosmic fire once again nears the earth. The planets are in a position to create a new dawning for mankind. But, there will be many cataclysms that will happen before the new era arrives. Mankind must again be tested to discover if the spirit has progressed sufficiently. Even now, the subterranean fire seeks to unite with the celestial elements of Akasa. The good forces must combine their power throughout the world, else the greatest catastrophes are destined to occur in the world.'

If Shamballah exists as a reality on or within the earth, why has not some adventurous explorer discovered a route to this fabled city? Roerich was puzzled by this same enigma and he mentioned that most heights have been explored, most valleys mapped, marked, and surveyed. 'Why hasn't someone found a route to Shamballah?' he inquired.

'There is gold within the earth and diamonds and rubies in the mountains,' said the lama. 'People are eager to possess these precious gifts and many people attempt to find them. To date, people have not discovered all things on this earth. So, let no man try to reach Shamballah without being called. You have heard the stories of poisoned streams which have deadly gasses emitting from their vaporous surface. Have you ever perceived how animals and humans tremble when they reach certain localities? Many people have tried to reach Shamballah – people who have been uncalled. Some of these people have vanished forever. A few have found the holy place, which indicated their Karma was ready.'

'Few people can understand the thoughts of people,' continued the lama. 'And those who can do so are silent! Have you ever met strangers during your travels, simply dressed strangers, who walk quietly through the heat or cold toward some unknown goal? Never believe that because their garment is simple any stranger is insignificant. It is an impossibility for man to determine from which direction a powerful presence may approach.'

'Tell me about the three monasteries near Lhasa – Sera, Depung, and Ganden.'

The lama leaned back against his ornate chair. His yellowed, wrinkled skin stretched like aged parchment into a thin smile. 'There are many holy monks in each monastery,' he said.

Roerich shook his head. 'I'm sure each monastery has holy men. Are there hidden tunnels under the Potala monastery? Can you tell me if there is a subterranean lake beneath one of these chief temples?'

The aged Tibetan smiled indulgently at his visitor. 'You are aware of so many things that I wonder if you have not come from Lhasa,' he remarked. 'If you have seen the subterranean lake you are either a very great lama, or a servant trained to guide holy men there by torchlight.

'Neither,' Roerich replied, 'but I have heard of these wonderous placese. Lama, have you met the Azaras?'

'You are familiar with many events. You must be a very successful man in your country,' the lama said, following a moment's meditation. 'To know so much about Shamballah is to have bathed in the stream of purification. Many of our people during their lives have met the Azaras and the snow people who serve them. Only in recent times have the Azaras quit coming into our cities. They are said to be settled now somewhere in the mountains. They are very tall, very erect, people with long hair and beards. Outwardly, they appear to look like a Hindu. The Azaras are the holy people who hold the secrets of Shamballah. Once, when I was walking in the mountains, I saw one of these chosen people. When I tried to run toward him, he turned beyond a rock and simply vanished. Yet, I found no cave or cavern where he might have hidden. Even the snow people do not appear in these times.'

It was the lama's turn to question his visitor. 'Do you in the Western world know of the magic stick which reveals the subterranean treasures of the earth?' he inquired.

'We have heard many stories of the unusual moving stick,' said Roerich. 'I understand that this magical scepter enables a man to find lost mines, underground springs, and water.'

'Who is the most important element in these experiments? The man or the stick?'

Roerich pursed his lips as he reflected on the question. 'The stick has no life, but man is brimming with vibration and magnetic power,' he replied. 'The stick is like a pen in the hand of a man.'

'All things are concentrated in the human body,' related the lama. 'The key is the knowledge of how to use it – not how to abuse it. Do you Westerners know of the great stone? The stone which possesses magic powers? Do you know that this stone came from another planet? Do you know who possessed this fabulous treasure?'

Roerich said he had heard legends of such stones. 'These stories go back to the time of the Druids. They tell of a great natural energy contained in this stone.'

'Do you have a name for the stone?'

'*Lapis Exilis* is the name of the stone.' Nicholas Roerich twisted in his chair. 'Have you talked with many Christian missionaries, lama?'

The old man gathered his robe around his thin body, seeking to keep away the evening chill. 'Your missionaries have visited our temples in centuries past,' he said, quietly. 'Those who have visited Lhasa told us of many marvelous tales. We knew some of these stories because some of the books of your religions are sealed in our libraries. We may know more about your religions than you realize. We have seen many missionaries in the past few years – they speak of one

Christ, but they speak ill of one another. Does Western man think that we are ignorant? We know that the rites practiced by one sect of Christians are not recognized by other Christians. Therefore, your priests must have many Christs.'

In another chapter of *Shamballah* entitled 'Subterranean Dwellers,' author Roerich informed his readers of the worldwide belief in the hollow earth and underground kingdoms. 'The subject of great migrations is the most fascinating in the history of humanity,' he wrote. 'What spirit was it that thus moved whole nations and innumerable tribes? What cataclysm drove the hordes from their familiar steppes? What new happiness and privileges did they anticipate in the blue mists of the desert.'

Roerich told of noticing similar carvings on rocks in the Himalaya mountains of Asia, in Mongolia, Siberia, and 'finally the same creative psychology in the halristningars of Sweden and Norway.' He mentioned that he had discovered these same ancient patterns carved into the stones of early Romanesque ruins.

A paradoxical man, Roerich was a trained archeologist who felt there was an underlying truth in folk tales and old legends. He wrote:

> Among the innumerable legends and fairy tales of various countries may be found the tales of lost tribes or subterranean dwellers. In wide and diverse directions, people are speaking of identical facts. But in correlating them you can readily see that these are but chapters from the one story. At first it seems impossible that there should exist any connection between these distorted whispers under the light of the desert bonfires. But afterward you begin to grasp a peculiar coincidence in these manifold legends by people who are even ignorant of each others' names.
>
> You recognize the same relationship in the folklores of Tibet, Mongolia, China, Turkestan, Kashmir, Persia, Altia, Siberia, the Ural, Caucasia, the Russian steppes, Lithu-

ania, Poland, Hungary, France, Germany; from the highest mountains to the deepest oceans . . . They tell how a holy tribe was persecuted by a tyrant and how the people, not willing to submit to cruelty, closed themselves into subteranean mountains. They even ask you if you want to see the entrance of the cave through which the saintly folk fled.

During his travels through the most unexplored areas of the Himalayan mountains, Roerich discovered many mysterious structures. Guides had been sent ahead one evening to set up a camp. When Roerich and his heavily-laden porters arrived at the encampment, it was built around a flat area some sixteen-thousand-feet high in the mountains. The camp site was near a stone ruin, described as similar to the Druid ruins at Stonehenge or Carnac. The stone ruins were composed of giant, long stones, so familiar to archeologists who have studied the vast ruins of ancient races. The Tibetan guides had no knowledge of who might have constructed the unusual rock structure. They simply said the site was sacred, a holy place where no one was allowed to excavate.

One of the most amazing, most controversial women in the annals of the occult is Madame Blavatsky, who is credited with founding *The Theosophical Society*. She claimed to be a magician, wizard, occultist, prophet, and a pupil of the 'Masters of Wisdom.' Born Helen Petrovna Hahn in a small village in the Russian Ukraine on July 31, 1831, she claimed to be ten years old when the mysterious 'Masters' began to talk with her. At the age of ten, the young girl told her aunt: '. . . There have always existed wise men who have all the knowledge of the world. They have total command over the forces of nature and they make themselves known only to those persons who are deemed worthy of knowing and seeing them. A person must also believe in them before you see them.'

At age seventeen, a marriage was arranged between the

young girl and General Blavatsky, a commander of the czar's armies. She lived with the aged military man less than three weeks. She left to travel the world for three decades. 'Love is a nightmare – a vile dream,' she recorded in her diary. 'Woman finds her true happiness in acquiring supernatural powers.'

Her years of travel are veiled in mystery. Her theosophical followers believe the fabulous occultist leader traveled in virtually every country of the world. She is supposed to have gone to Egypt, where she held a midnight seance in the Queen's Chamber of the Great Pyramid at Giza, Egypt. She performed rites and chanted incantations to raise the ancient spirits of long-dead Egyptian priests. Later, she was in India where she became engrossed with the magical performances of the Asian wizards. Finally, clad in the garments of a man, she is supposed to have visited several of the monasteries of Tibet. In 1874, she founded *The Theosophical Society*. This group was founded to 'lead men to their true spiritual nature'.

Madame Blavatsky's greatest literary work is *The Secret Doctrine*, one of the most remarkable occult books ever published. In *The Secret Doctrine* she told of ancient, subterranean tunnels, underground cities, and hidden depositories of ancient literature. The book was published shortly before her death on May 8, 1891. Selections related to the hollow earth mystery include:

> Moreover in all of the large and wealthy Lamaseries, there are subterranean crypts and cave-libraries, cut in the rock, where the Gonpa and the Ihakhang are situated in the mountains. Beyond the western Tsaydam, in the solitary passes of Kuen-len, there are several such hiding places. Along the ridge of Altyn-tag, whose soil no European foot has ever trodden so far, there exists a certain hamlet, lost in a deep gorge. It is a small cluster of houses, a hamlet rather than a monastery, with a poor-looking temple in it, and one old lama, a hermit, living near to

watch it. Pilgrims say that the subterranean galleries and halls under it contain a collection of books, the number of which, according to the accounts given, is too large to find room even in the British museum.

According to the same tradition the now desolate regions of the waterless land of Tamin – a virtual wilderness in the heart of Turkestan – were in days of old covered with flourishing and wealthy cities. At present, a few verdant oases only relieve its dread solitude. One such, carpeting the sepulchre of a vast city buried under the sandy soil of the desert, belongs to no one, but is often visited by Mongolians and Buddhists. The tradition also speaks of immense subterranean abodes of large corridors filled with tiles and cylinders ...'

Madame Blavatsky based her published reports on statements from people she had met during her travels. She admitted that the subterranean crypts and underground cities might well be 'actual fact' or 'idle rumor'.

Beasts, Men and Gods (E. P. Dutton & Co., New York, 1922) is another remarkable book containing information on the hollow earth mystery. Author Ferdinand Ossendowski also tells of Asian legends of Agharta. An excerpt from that book is reproduced here:

On my journey into Central Asia I came to know for the first time about the 'Mystery of Mysteries', which I can call by no other name. At the outset I did not pay very much attention to it and did not attach to it such importance as I afterwards realized belonged to it, when I had analyzed and connoted many sporadic, hazy, and often controversial bits of evidence.

The old people on the shore of the river Amyl related to me an ancient legend to the effect that a certain Mongolian tribe in their escape from the demands of Genghis Khan hid themselves in the subterranean country. Afterward, a Soyot from near the Lake of Nogan Kul showed me the smoking gate that serves as the entrance to the 'Kingdom of Agharta'. Through this gate a hunter formerly entered into the Kingdom and, after his return, began to relate what he had seen there. The lamas cut out his tongue in order to prevent him from telling about the Mystery of Mysteries. When he arrived at old age, he came back to the entrance to this cave and disappeared into the subterranean kingdom, the memory of which had ornamented and lightened his nomad heart.

I received more realistic information about this from Hutuktu Jelyb Djamsrap, in Narabanchi Kure. He told of the semi-realistic arrival of the powerful King of the World from the subterranean kingdom, of his appearance, his miracles and of his prophecies; and only then did I begin to understand that in that legend, hypnosis or mass vision, is hidden not only the mystery but a realistic and powerful force capable of influencing the political life of Asia. From that moment I began making some investigations.

The favorite Gelong Lama of Prince Chultan Beyli and the Prince himself gave me an account of the subterranean kingdom.

'Everything in the world,' said Gelong, 'is constantly in a state of change and transition – peoples, science, religions, laws, and customs. How many great empires and brilliant cultures have perished! And that alone which remains unchanged is Evil, the tool of the Bad Spirits. More than sixty thousand years ago a Holyman disappeared with a whole tribe of people under the ground and never appeared again on the surface of the earth ... Many people have visited this kingdom ... (but ... no one knows where this place is, Some say Afghanistan, others India. All the people there are protected against Evil and crimes do not exist within its bournes. Science has developed calmly and nothing is threatened with destruction. The subterranean people have reached the highest knowledge. Now it is a large kingdom, millions of men with the King of the World as their ruler. He knows all the forces of the world and reads all the souls of humankind and the great book of their destiny. Invisibly he rules eight million men on the surface of the earth and they will accomplish his every order.'

Prince Chultan Beyli added: 'This kingdom is Agharta. It extends throughout all the subterannean passages of the whole world. I heard a learned lama of China relating to Bogdo Khan that all the subterranean caves of America are inhabited by an ancient people who have disappeared underground. Traces of them are still found on the surface of the land. These subterranean peoples and spaces are governed by rulers owing allegiance to the King of the World. In it there is not much of the wonderful. You know that in the two greatest oceans of the east and the west were formerly two continents. They disappeared under the water but their people went into the subterranean kingdom. In the underground caves there exists a peculiar light which affords growth to the grains and vegetables and long life without disease to the people. There are many different peoples and many different tribes. An old Buddhist Brahman in Nepal was carrying out the will of the Gods in making a visit to the ancient kingdom of Jenghiz – Siam – where he met a fisherman who ordered him to take a place in his boat and sail with him upon the sea. On the third day they reached an island where he met a people having two tongues which could speak separately in different languages. They showed to him peculiar, unfamiliar animals, tortoises with sixteen feet and one eye, huge snakes with a very tasty flesh and birds with teeth which caught fish for their masters in the sea. These people told him that they had come up out of the subterranean kingdom and described to him certain parts of the underground country.'

The Lama Turgut traveling with me from Urga to Peking gave me further details.

The capital of Agharta is surrounded with towns of high priests and scientists. It reminds one of Lhasa where the palace of the Dalai Lama, the Potala, is the top of a mountain covered with monasteries and temples. The throne of the King of the World is surrounded by millions of incarnated Gods. They are the Holy Panditas. The palace itself is encircled by the palaces of the Goro, who possess all the visible and invisible forces of the earth, of inferno and of the sky and who can do everything for the life and death of man. If our mad humankind should begin to war against them, they would be able to explode the whole surface of our planet and transform it into deserts. They can dry up the seas, transform lands into oceans and scatter the mountains into the sands of the deserts. By his order trees, grasses and bushes can be made to grow; old and feeble men can become young and stalwart; and the dead can be resurrected. In cars strange and unknown to us they rush through the narrow cleavages inside our planet. Some Indian Brahmans and Tibetan Dalai Lamas during their laborious struggles to the peaks of mountains which no other human feet had trod have found there inscriptions carved on the rocks, footprints in the snow and the tracks of wheels. The blissful Sakkia Mouni found on one mountain top tablets of stone carrying words which he only understood in his old age and afterward penetrated into the Kingdom of Agharta, from which he brought back crumbs of the sacred learning preserved in his memory. There in palaces of wonderful crystal live the invisible rulers of all pious people, the King of the World or Brahytma, who can speak with God as I speak with you, and his two assistants, Mahytma, knowing the purposes of future events, and Mahynga, ruling the causes of these events.

The Holy Panditas study the world and all its forces. Sometimes the most learned among them collect together and send envoys to that place where the human eyes have never penetrated. This is described by the Tashi Lama living eight hundred and fifty years ago. The highest Panditas place their hands on their eyes and at the base of the brain of younger ones and force them into a deep sleep, wash their bodies with an infusion of grass and make them immune to pain and harder than stones, wrap them in magic cloths, bind them and then pray to the Great God. The petrified youths lie with eyes and ears open and alert, seeing, hearing and remembering everything. Afterwards a Goro approaches and fastens a long, steady gaze upon them. Very slowly the bodies lift themselves from the earth and disappear. The Goro sits and stares with fixed eyes to the place whither he has sent them. Invisible threads join them to his will. Some of them course among the stars, observe their events, their unknown peoples, their life and their laws. They listen to their talk, read their books, understand their fortunes and woes, their holiness and sins, their piety and evil. Some are mingled with flame and see the creature of fire, quick and ferocious, eternally fighting, melting and hammering metals in the depths of planets, boiling the water for geysers and springs, melting the rocks and pushing out molten streams over the surface of the earth through the holes in the mountains. Others rush together with the ever elusive, infinitesimally small, transparent creatures of the air and penetrate into the mysteries of their existence and into the purposes of their life. Others slip into the depths of the seas and observe the kingdom of the wise creatures of the water, who transport and spread genial warmth all over the earth, ruling the winds, waves and storms . . . In Erdeni Dzu formerly lived Pandita Hutuktu, who had come from Agharta. As he was dying, he told about the time when he lived according to the will of the Goro on a red star in the east, floated in the ice-covered ocean and flew among the stormy fires in the depths of the earth.

These are the tales which I heard in the Mongolian

yurtas of Princes and in the Lamaite monasteries. These stories were all related in a solemn tone which forbade challenge and doubt.

Mystery . . .

DOC ANDERSON – PYRAMIDS, TUNNELS, AND TIBET

One of the few people in America to have personally investigated the Buddhist belief in a hollow earth is R. C. 'Doc' Anderson, 302 Gordon Avenue, Rossville, Georgia. Anderson is an impressive, internationally acclaimed psychic, seer, and clairvoyant. He has counseled people for more than three decades from his ESP studio, located across the Georgia state line from Chattanooga, Tennessee. A six-foot-two-inch, three-hundred-pound giant, Doc Anderson has been called 'a living Edgar Cayce,' 'a modern Nostradamus,' and his biography and book of predictions for the future was entitled *The Man Who Sees Tomorrow* (Paperback Library; New York; 1970).

Whatever his title, Anderson's unusual ability to predict the future is well documented. The southern seer makes his predictions to the public, in print, or on television, prior to the actual event. He was the subject of a recent study on prophetic tests and the investigation revealed that Doc Anderson rated an impressive 91.34 per cent accuracy in predictions for his clients.

Although he is now in his early sixties, Doc Anderson has the strength and robust health of a much younger person. In his youth, he toured the world and earned his way as a prizefighter, wrestler, bullfighter, merchant seaman, and showman.

'It was during my trips to the Orient that I became aware of the legend of the Hollow Earth,' Doc Anderson revealed. 'I heard of Agharta, a kingdom located inside the earth. I first heard in Tibet about the King of the World. I was a young, happy-go-lucky vagabond in those days. I had the strength of several men. I had the curiosity of a dozen children. A buddy of mine was very good at handling foreign languages and dialects. We wanted to see everything in the world. Before we settled down, we'd seen everything that can be imagined – and maybe just a little bit more.'

Anderson's psychic talents were responsible for his travels. These impressive gifts were first manifested when he was a young boy, living at his family home in Granger, Iowa, in 1918. 'I had always been very close to my brother, Nelson,' Anderson recalled. 'He had left home to join the Canadian Army. He was in Europe fighting in the bloody trenches against the Germans.'

Anderson was playing on the floor of the family living room when he was strangely drawn to a picture of his brother on the wall. 'Something compelled me to stare at that picture of Nels,' Anderson said. 'I was conscious of a strange feeling that flowed through me. Without warning, I was given a very vivid vision of Nels dashing across a battlefield. Suddenly, he was wounded in the face by a bullet. I knew it was a fatal wound before he slumped back onto the ground.' As the vision ended, the glass shattered over Nelson Anderson's picture and dropped to the floor.

Little Bobby Anderson ran to his mother in the kitchen. 'Nels is dead!' he cried. 'Nels has been shot!'

Mrs. Anderson slapped the frightened boy across the face. Her fingers dug into his shoulders as she shook him. 'Don't think such thoughts, Bobby!' she pleaded. 'Don't say something like that about your brother.'

Unfortunately, the young man's prediction proved true. A telegram arrived a few days afterward from the Canadian Army, announcing the death of Nelson Anderson. The young soldier had been hit in the face by a sniper's bullet. 'That experience left a terrible impression on my mind. I grew up trying to forget my psychic gifts,' Doc Anderson related. 'The trauma of that vision haunted me for many years. I didn't know if these gifts to foretell the future were God's will – or a curse placed on me by the devil. I never asked to be gifted with ESP, which was known as second sight in those days. I simply wanted to live a normal life.

People who had ESP in those days were often considered a bit unusual, a little strange.'

As he grew into manhood, Anderson developed a curiosity about psychic abilities. 'As I knocked around the world, I visited with people who were experts on the subject,' he related. 'My buddy and I were interested in everything, but we had the greatest curiosity about the unknown.'

Anderson and his friend, Frank Shearer, signed aboard a merchant ship that sailed to India. 'That marvelous land was under British rule in those days,' the phychic said. 'We earned our way by performing shows at the various British army posts. I was strong enough in those days to pick up one end of an automobile. We always got a great reception wherever we went. In one little outpost, I made my entrance on stage carrying a pony on my back.'

While he was in India, Anderson and his friend heard about the Himalayan mountains and the mysterious lands beyond those snowy peaks. 'We gathered up camping equipment and an old colonel gave us a pass that was good on any railroad out there,' Anderson said. 'We took off for the land beyond the mountains.'

In those days the isolated regions of China, Mongolia, and Tibet were ruled by ferocious war-lords. These feudal-like chieftains paid homage to no king or government. 'They were a government in themselves,' Anderson related. 'They had their own armies, their servants, followers, and they collected taxes at the point of a gun barrel. They lived – and died – by the might of their armies. Some of these war-lords had thousands of men in their armies, yet they were little more than bandits. We relied on my strength as a strongman, and Frank's quick wits and ready tongue, to keep us out of trouble. Nevertheless, on a couple of occasions, we almost lost our heads. I mean that just as it sounds because they executed their enemies over there by beheading them with a big, giant sword.'

Asia was in turmoil in those times. War-lords ruled the outer regions, demanding fees from land-owners and villages. The land was brimming with monks, monastery abbots, 'white' Russian refugees, and mustached Tartars who had escaped the Communists in Russia with their wives, families, and cattle. Soldiers-of-fortune and adventurers wandered through the Far East in search of wealth, security, or a warm place to rest for a few days. 'Frank was quick on languages so we got along with most everyone,' Anderson said. 'He had a natural talent for talking with anyone. He'd meet a tribesman from the Gobi desert and, within a few hours, he'd know the dialect.'

Anderson's first contact with the legend of the Hollow Earth occurred during his travels through Tibet. 'We were thinking of going to Lhasa, the capital city, to seek an audience with the Living Buddha,' the psychic explained. 'We were coming out of the Sinkiang province of China. A bunch of the war-lords had gotten into a squabble there. They were killing each other off with angry Oriental vengeance. We decided that getting away from there was the best way to stay alive.'

Anderson and Shearer were walking along a lonely trail that led to Lhasa. 'Suddenly, from behind us, we heard the loud blast of a trumpet,' the psychic related. 'We looked back and, buddy, believe it or not, an automobile was coming down that road. It was a beat-up, old Stanley Steamer pulled by a couple of oxen. In the car was the fattest war-lord of all times. He was dressed in fur clothes they wear over there and he was drunk on Asian moonshine. We learned he was the local war-lord.'

The war-lord's caravan drew abreast of the two Americans. 'He was the only one allowed in the car,' Anderson said. 'His wives and children walked. This old chief was not the kind of man who believed in Women's Liberation.'

The mongol greeted the weary Americans with a wide grin and an eager hug. 'He was tickled to see us,' Anderson continued. 'The old guy had killed someone for that Stanley Steamer. It was his pride and joy and one of his monks was the chief mechanic. The mechanic wasn't keeping the car running.

'Their method of fixing the car was wild,' Anderson chuckled. 'The monk placed a few people around the car with sticks. On signal, everyone tried to beat the car into running. After that, the monk prayed to the King of the World to repair the old steamer. Needless to say, the King never appeared.'

Frank Shearer was a mechanically-minded young man. We dug some tools out of the car,' the seer related. 'In a couple of hours, the boilers were filled, and the car was running. The war-lord apparently just ran it at one particular place; he insisted that we accompany him to his local drag strip.'

The car was shut off and the oxen were once again hooked to the vehicle. 'We started out across the country,' Anderson said. 'We were about half way there when the war-lord gave a shout and the caravan stopped.'

The camels and horses were drawn into a tight cluster and their halters tied to the car. An eerie silence descended over the Asian plains. The animals whinnied with apprehension as the war-lord and his followers looked around the area.

'The King of the World is speaking!' proclaimed the mongol. He clasped his hands in prayer and faced the mountains. 'The one who watches over all will speak.'

The incredulous Americans watched as their hosts repeated the sacred phrase of *'Om! Om! Mani Padme Huang!'* The monks in the caravan turned their prayer wheels, shouting the words down toward the ground.

'What's going on?' Anderson inquired. He turned to his partner. 'What's happening?'

'Om! Om!' chanted the mongols. *'Om! Mani Padme Huang!'* Hail to the great Lama of the lotus flower!

After several minutes of fervent prayer, the group rested before resuming their journey. The monk, who wore a red robe with yellow sashes, explained the incident to the two white men. 'All living things must cease their activity when the King of the World prays for the destiny of people,' the monk said. 'Those of us who live on the surface must join with the King of the World in praying for the deliverance of everything on earth.'

'Where does this King live?' asked Frank Shearer.

'In his magnificent city in the underground.' The monk pointed his finger down toward the earth. 'There are marvelous cities beneath the earth, subterranean kingdoms where the Blessed Ones live in paradise.'

'How do you get to these cities?'

'The old lamas know the way,' replied the monk. 'It is not a secret that is entrusted to unworthy ones. I have heard there is a tunnel that runs down to Agharta, the Holy Place. These tunnels connect up with certain of the ancient monasteries in Lhasa.'

Doc Anderson and Frank Shearer dismissed the story as simply another Oriental superstition. 'We continued on our journey and reached a flat, level plain in mid-afternoon,' Anderson said. 'The monk was excited because he interpreted the message from the King of the World as indicating pleasure that we had joined his band. The following morning, he woke us up early, sounded the trumpet, and announced he would run the Stanley Steamer across the plain. Both Frank and I figured he would test the car, so Frank helped get up a batch of steam in the car. The war-lord got in the vehicle and – whoosh! – off he went across the flatlands. Racing faster and faster, and not holding back on the steam. A Stanley Steamer could run like the wind and he kept it wide open. There was a ridge about three miles from the encampment and, over it he went, pressing for more steam"

Anderson and the mongolians became alarmed when the Stanley Steamer's wheels left the ground in going over the small enbankment. 'Ohmigosh! He's killed himself,' blurted out Frank Shearer. He ran toward the horizon.

'The war-lord's horsemen got there first and, shortly afterward, they came in sight over the bank, pulling the Stanley Steamer with their lassos,' Anderson continued. 'The old chief was a terrible sight. He'd hit the ridge and the car leaped into the air. He was thrown out when it hit the ground. He was lucky to be alive. Later, we found out he had driven the car only once before. He pleaded with Frank to start it again, but Frank made a deal with the monk. The monk interpreted the message from the King of the World to say it meant the old man should never drive again.'

Anderson and Shearer remained with the war-lord for several weeks, then slipped away from the camp one night. 'He kept bothering Frank to fix up the car,' the psychic explained. 'Even more frightening, buddy, he decided I should marry his oldest daughter. He really wanted to hold a wedding. That girl was about five feet tall, weighed at least three hundred pounds, and she smelled like a goat. Plus, she looked as if she'd been hit in the face by a hundred hammers.'

The two adventurous young men talked about the King of the World and the alleged subterranean paradise as they continued their travels. 'We started asking about it,' Anderson said. 'Some people talked openly about it. A few claimed to know where a tunnel entrance was hidden, a route direct to the secret city. Yet, we could never find anyone who really knew where it was. A lot of the monks guarded their tongues when we mentioned the subject, so we decided to visit a couple of their highest pontiffs of their church-state to ask about it.'

At that time, the most important lama was living in the palace at Lhasa, Tibet's capital city. The Dalai Lama was worshipped as the God-king of Tibet, and the spiritual and temporal leader of millions of faithful Mahayana Buddhists. He was considered to be an incarnation of Buddha.

Another important religious and political leader was the Tashi Lama. His spiritual domain crossed the national boundaries of Mongolia, Tibet, and Manchuria, and extended into portions of India. 'The Tashi Lama reigned from a monastery at Kumbum, in northeast Tibet,' Anderson related. 'He was the second most powerful man in all of Asia.' Another High Lama ruled portions of Mongolia from Urga, the capital city of that isolated country.

'Several times we were told by the bogdos, the Holy Ones, that the mystery of the subterranean kingdom would be solved when the seven pyramids of Shensi were opened,' Anderson drawled in a deep, southern accent. 'One old bogdo was a good friend of ours. We'd heard of the pyramids of Egypt, buddy, but pyramids in Asia were something else again. These pyramids were in a westerly direction from Sian-fu, the capital of Shensi province.'

The two young men traveled along the great caravan road that stretches from Peking, China, to the shores of the Mediterranean sea. 'We asked about the pyramids at each village,' Anderson said. 'Frank couldn't speak the local dialect, but there was usually a chief in each place who knew pure Chinese. At one place, an old man said the pyramids were a couple of days' travel from his village.'

The caravan trail was simply a dirt road that had been trodden into the earth by generations of traders. Spices, rare perfumes, and the treasures of the East had been carried by camels along the trail. 'Orientals are not surprised about pyramids being located in Asia,' Doc Anderson recalled. 'They're secure in the knowledge that they have been gifted by the gods with divine illumination. The Bogdos believe they are the direct descendents of the world's first priestly caste. They believed that Tibet and the Asian highlands was the oldest land in the world and, after seeing some of their ancient records and documents, I am inclined to agree.'

The land around the pyramids was a long, desolate flatland. The entire region was under cultivation and forested areas had been cleared away. There were seven pyramids, flat-topped, with three giants resting along the outer edges. 'There was a tiny village about two miles from the large pyramid,' Anderson related. 'We asked the old lama there about the pyramids, but he could only shake his head. They were another of the mysteries of Asia. The pyramids were mentioned in ancient scrolls in the temples. He believed they were at least 5,000 – perhaps 6,000 – years old. No one knows for certain who built them, why they were constructed, or how they were built out on this flat plain.'

Anderson, Frank Shearer, and the lama walked out to inspect the largest pyramid. 'It may be the largest man-made structure on earth,' Doc drawled. 'We estimated it was about 2,000 feet at the base and about 1,200 feet high. This makes the Asian structure twice as large as the largest pyramid in Egypt.' (Anderson visited Egypt's pyramids at Giza in 1970 and believes he is the only man now living to have seen both the Asian and Egyptian structures.)

'We had a compass and discovered the four faces of the pyramids were lined up with the compass points. They were very precise in their work,' the southern seer related. 'There were a few remains of colors on the sides, indicating colors were given to each side. The east was aqua-green; the south was red, and black was for the west. The color of the northern sides was white. These pyramids had a flat top and there was traces of yellow up there.'

The monk grinned with delight as Anderson and his companion gazed with awed respect at the giant pyramid. 'Do you believe that foreign white devils are the only intelligent people?' the monk inquired.

'Someone sure knew what they were doing,' replied the incredulous young man.

'I wonder who they were,' said Frank Shearer.

The monk shrugged his shoulders. 'The oldest books in the monasteries claim they were old when those scrolls were written. No one really knows about them.'

'Why hasn't someone tried to open them up?'

'Perhaps we will do it someday,' said the monk. 'There is plenty of time to do it. We have all of eternity.'

'Has a white man ever seen them before?' Doc Anderson asked.

'A few. The village chieftain said a white devil was through here when he was a little boy.'

Doc Anderson continued to stare at the impressive structures. 'Doesn't anyone know about these things,' he chided. 'Surely, somewhere in this country there's a person who knows something about them.'

'The most powerful lama, the Living Buddha, might know,' replied the monk, 'but I doubt that he will tell the secrets to white devils.'

'What do you think about them?' Frank Shearer inquired.

'That the secrets of the King of the World are stored within,' the monk said. 'The oldest records of our people, the people before them, and those before them, are stored here. In time, and when the King of the World announces his presence, these places will be opened.'

'What about the story an old Bogdo told me,' Anderson inquired. 'He said there were tunnel entrances beneath these pyramids. The tunnels are said to connect up with the pyramids in Egypt, the highest monasteries, and they run under the oceans to connect every land.'

'I would not know,' said the monk. 'It is enough to look at them and wonder. One should not be too curious. One should not try to reach the paradise below. I have heard of those who tried and they disappeared.'

The sun was sinking below the horizon as the three men walked away from the monumental structures. 'I never saw or heard of those pyramids again until back in the early nineteen fifties,' Doc Anderson revealed. 'A magazine printed a story about them. A few old boys down here had kidded me over the years about my mythical Asian pyramids. I had a bit of fun chiding them when my assistant ran across the article. It included a picture of the pyramids taken from a U.S. Army airplane in 1946. It still looked as immense as ever, buddy, and I was glad to have a little proof that I wasn't telling tall tales. Then, the Communists took over those lands and I've never heard about those big man-made mountains since then.'

During their visits to the lamasery at Lhasa and Kumbum, Doc Anderson sought out historians for the Living Gods. 'The Red God allowed me to stumble around in their library,' he stated. 'Buddy, they record every day in a big book. They have a history that runs back thousands of years. Those monks use little brushes which are dipped in ink. They're real wizards at writing down things. Some of those old scrolls and books were said to be about ten thousand years old. I've always been sorry that I couldn't read them. I just went to the eighth grade and I was lucky to be able to read the American language. That stuff just looked like so many Chinese laundry tickets to me.'

At one of the sacred monasteries, Anderson and Shearer were shown a porcelain casket that contained several clay tablets and discs. 'They were filled with markings, as if someone had pressed a sharp point into the clay when it was wet,' Doc said. 'There were various pictures inscribed on the clay, including those of several pyramids.'

'These tablets are at least 20,000 years old,' announced the lama.

'May I touch it?' Anderson asked.

'Of course,' replied the amused lama. 'They are in excellent condition.'

Tenderly, the young American placed one of his large fingers down upon the edge of a tablet.

'No one else from across the big waters has ever done that,' announced the lama.

'What do they say?' Frank Shearer eyed the tablets with undisguised curiosity.

'These tell about the people who lived in a land in the center of the great water,' explained the holy man. 'They built temples, traded with our ancestors, and built the pyramids you mentioned.'

'Who were they?'

The lama shook his head sadly. 'No one knows,' he explained. 'There are other tablets in our library that tell of how their land disappeared beneath the waters. A holy leader led them through the tunnels and down to Agharta. They lived in Shamballah with the King of the World.'

'Do the pyramids mark the entrance to the tunnels?' Doc Anderson inquired.

'Among other things,' said the lama. 'There are markings throughout the world to indicate the tunnel entrances. But the markings are revealed only to those who should know them. Have you not seen strange symbols engraved on the sides of mountains? Have you not wondered about the unusual engravings that have been cut in rocks in the past? The ignorant ignore these things and dismiss them. Those who seek the tunnel entrances recognize them as signs that lead to Shamballah, the capital of Agharta.'

At that same monastery in Kumbum, Anderson was given the secrets of telepathic travel. 'Son, some of those old monks have mental power beyond our comprehension,' he drawled. 'They can project their minds to and fro into the past or future. They're quite a bunch. Professors used to laugh at stories of their abilities, but now they're starting to test them under scientific conditions in psychological laboratories. The people who used to laugh are now discovering the limitless potential of the human mind. Buddy, we can do almost anything if we cut out bad thoughts and negative thinking. All things are available to those who know the route. The way is always revealed to the truthful seeker.'

In an interview at his ESP studio in Rossville, Georgia, I questioned Doc Anderson about the legends of the hollow earth. This is a transcript of that conversation:

Were you ever given an audience with the Dalai Lama, the Living Buddha?

DOC ANDERSON: We finally got to Lhasa near the end of our adventures. The Dalai Lama lived there in a magnificent monastery, attended by several hundred servants, monks, and assistants. Our audience was arranged by an Englishman, the pontiff's physician. The Englishman had greeted us like brothers when we came walking into the holy city. He had been in the king's army in India, gotten into some sort of scrape, and took off for Tibet. I think he may have been a murderer, as he said he could never return to civilization again. You didn't ask too much of people out there in those times. He was tickled to death to see a white face, someone who could talk the English language.

The first thing you notice about a Tibetan home, building, or monastery is the odor. Those people never took a bath unless they happened to fall in a river. They didn't have a system of disposing of their garbage or sewerage. On the one hand, they lived in incredible poverty with no physical refinements. Yet, they were spiritually advanced on the mental level. I was always confused by the contrast.

Was this a personal audience with the Dalai Lama?

DOC ANDERSON: We had spent a few days in Lhasa and requested an audience. We were guests of the Englishman, who lived away from the lamasery. Eventually, word came by courier that the Living Buddha would be pleased to see Frank and me. He was very amused by our appearance and eagerly asked us about our travels throughout the world.

The Englishman was there with us and we were watched by a *kanpo*, abbot of the lamasery. The *kanpo* also acted as the official food taster for the Living Buddha. Tibet had a number of black monks, who were dedicated to the destruction of the red and yellow faiths. Some of the black monks were always trying to poison the highest leaders of the other faiths. Buddy, poison was a constant danger in Tibet and Mongolia. There was a fellow known as a *tzuren*, who is sort of a combination doctor and poisoner. If you hired them as a doctor, they would probably cure you if it was in their power. Unless, of course, they'd been paid more to kill you. I also knew of a *tzuren* who became known throughout Tibet as a fearful practitioner of poisons. He slipped a slow acting poison to his victims, a rare Oriental concoction. He provided an antidote for a big price. You could tell a lot of these fellows if you watched for the sign of the swastika;

this was their symbol of power. Later, Hitler made it an even more terrible symbol.

What was the Living Buddha like in person?

DOC ANDERSON: He was a surprisingly young man. He was well educated, courteous, and he had a sense of humor. His one wish was someday to ride in an airplane. He told us that the old records in the monastery told of people who had swooped down out of the skies in ancient times. He said these visitors had flying machines that zipped through the clouds and over the mountains. He said these same ships were now in Agharta, the subterranean kingdom.

Did he describe these airships?

DOC ANDERSON: We asked about them and a priest was sent to a library. He returned with an old book bound in animal hide and tied with leather thongs. There was a drawing of an egg-shaped device flying over a high mountain. Buddy, this was a very old book. I never saw another picture like that until drawings of UFOs and flying saucers popped up in the news after the war.

Did you learn anything new about the hollow earth belief?

DOC ANDERSON: The Englishman was really excited about that idea. He said there was a tunnel beneath the monastary that connected up with a world-wide network of tunnels. He claimed the treasures of Atlantis, and the secrets of the ages, were located in various treasure vaults under the earth.

The Englishman knew more about the Buddhist belief in Agharta than anyone we met. He was attempting to decipher some of the old writings and he maintained some thick notebooks on his work. He swore there were tunnels all over the world. According to him, this paradise was the ultimate place to live on this earth. He claimed it had been the Biblical Garden of Eden.

We were informed that the average monk, or priest, was not given information on the location of tunnel entrances. Beneath the monastery, in a dark dungeon, we were shown a light that has supposedly burned for thousands of years. The Englishman showed us a massive gold door that marked the entrance into the subterranean tunnels. He believed that representatives of the underworld came out of this tunnel to meet with the Living Buddha and his advisers.

What else were you told about the tunnels?

DOC ANDERSON: In Lhasa, those initiated into the highest doctrine were given the location of tunnel entrances. The Englishman felt there was an opening in Brazil, hyper-Brazil, he called it. There was supposed to be markings in other lands to indicate the location of another entrance. North America has several entrances and there's others scattered around the world.

We were told that the Pyramids all over the world are connected by these tunnels. The Englishman claimed one of those ancient airships was buried inside the Great Pyramid at Giza, Egypt. I was over there last year and, buddy, they're having a difficult time getting anything out of those old structures.

Did they say when the tunnels or pyramids would be opened?

DOC ANDERSON: There's a saying in the Orient that when the student is ready, a teacher will appear. That's the case with these things. They claimed that as man progresses up to a higher spiritual level, there will be certain truths delivered to him. They believe that humanity – you, me, everyone, buddy – must be able to handle this knowledge. The earth still holds many secrets and she holds them well.

Did you hear any legends about the King of the World?

DOC ANDERSON: He is the guiding light of the earth, according to the Buddhists. He is said to be known to all men in one form or another. They claim he is the highest developed, most perfect being on this planet. He is attuned to the All-knowing God of the universe. They believe he directs the essence of life, is the divine illumination behind all religions, and is the spokesman for cosmic power.

The King of the World is the fellow who is supposed to guide the *Panditas*, the highest rank of monks in the Buddhist order. He is also the boss of the *Goro*, an order of priests who live in their subterranean paradise. The *Goro* helps the King in directing humanity on the righteous course. They speak all languages and they have the power to read or direct minds. When they talk to each other, they speak *vatannan* – the secret language of the subterranean world.

Does the King of the World rule forever?

DOC ANDERSON: Nosiree, buddy. Just like everybody else he must undergo certain tests of purification. On those times, he annoints himself with selected oils and enters a secret cave that contains a cosmic temple. This cave has been in existence since the beginning of time. The embalmed body of the original King of the World lies in state at the end of the cave, in a magical casket of black stone.

The cave is always dark and, when he nears the entrance, the King of the World must make certain chants, perform rituals, and repeat his incantations. When these are completed, the cave entrance opens and the darkness disappears as the walls of the cave glow with a ruby light. At the same time, a dancing mass of flames leaps up from the body in the black stone coffin. Images appear on the glowing cave walls, the faces of *Goros* and High Priests who have gone over to the spirit world. These images are said to be extremely frightening because they are a projection of the earthly body as it exists at that precise moment. Many are simply mounds of dust. Others are mouldy skull faces, eaten away by earth and time. Still others are the fleshless skulls of the recent dead.

As the faces gleam on the glowing cave walls, they chant a higher version of '*Om*' to unleash the power of nature. The incantation creates an opening in the walls of the cave. Through this chasm comes two lines of skeleton men, shrouded in the colors of death and illuminated by a greenish light. The skeleton men form an aisle that leads back toward the coffin.

The King of the World must now walk slowly toward the black stone casket, through the alley of skeleton men, as a test of his faith and purity. As he walks toward the embalmed body of his predecessor, the king may be tested by any of the skeleton men. Questions asked by the skeleton men measure his humility, purity, faith, and enlightenment. The King may be tested once, thrice, or a thousand times as he walks towards the flaming body of the original king.

Once he has passed the tests, he remains in a sacred state of prayer before the flaming casket. At this precise moment, he is attuned with all of the souls throughout the world. He asks for guidance to assist humanity.

When that moment has passed, he must walk courageously up to the flames shooting out of the black casket and place his arms and hands inside the fire. They claim this is the hottest fire on earth. The fellow must remain there until the flesh has burned away from his bones. If he is still found worthy, then the flesh will be instantly returned to his hands and arms.

Tested and proven true, the flames disappear from the casket. The greenish light dims as the skeletons return to their eternal vault inside the cave walls. Multi-colored lights shoot out from the coffin, signaling that the King of the World is victorious and is purified to serve mankind.

As he walks back down the corridor in the cave, the images of the frightening *Goro* faces vanish. Finally, the entrance is closed, the sacred cave sealed, and the King goes forth to rule.

That sounds like something out of Edgar Allen Poe by way of Lovecraft. That's quite a legend.

Doc Anderson: I've met an awful lot of people who believe in it. I forgot to mention that the King is also given messages to guide his actions in the future. These are from the Council of Universal Karma. These messages are delivered when the entire assembly is in prayerful attunement with the thoughts of all men on this earthly plane. They probe the minds of influential people like kings, presidents, and world leaders. They read the plans of these people; they are judged by the council. All things are supposedly known to this tribunal.

What occurs after the deliberation?

DOC ANDERSON: Karmic destiny is in the balance and the Tibetans believe the King of the World will help those people who are righteous. In turn, those who act against the will of God are doomed to destruction. This power is directed, for good or destruction, under the science of '*Om*'. '*Om*' is a science of prayer based on Om, the name of the first *Goro* on earth. He is said to have been the most ancient of holy men. They believe he walked upon this earth many hundreds of thousands of years ago as the first person in tune with the infinite goodness of God. He was the first great Master Teacher, a great warrior against the forces of Evil. '*Om*' was given the power to direct all things in the visible world, due to his excellent service.

How are they supposed to carry out the judgments?

DOC ANDERSON: A council of Masters is called together at Agharta by the King of the World. These are the 'Masters' who sit in judgment to deliberate the purity and enlightenment of selected students. They determine whether an adept will be selected for guidance on a cosmic-psychic-material level.

What about the alleged forces of evil from the subterranean world?

DOC ANDERSON: Buddy, you can always be sure that where there is good, there will also be the evil ones. There is supposed to be a dark order in the under world, totally dedicated to the absolute destruction of surface mankind. These devilmen are allegedly capable of inflicting plagues, misfortune, and dreaded disease upon mankind. They can strike down an entire nation with a plague, an earthquake, or a disaster. These are supposed to be the demonic forces behind tyrants, dictators, and other brutal men in history.

These satanic legions are also supposed to be capable of focusing in on a single individual. They have the power of the hex. They can turn a man's opportunities to dust; every golden moment crumbles into dirt. In Tibet, if a wealthy man begins to lose his land, his wife, and family – well, they believe he has been hexed by the subterranean demons. He is a victim of the devilmen.

These afflictions and misfortunes can only be removed by the rituals of *Om* – the science of prayer. Until the hex is removed, few men will go near the victim. There is a superstition that the devilmen may see a more interesting victim and leave the original person. They think the best protection against the devilmen is to affix the sign of *obo* on themselves, and their possessions. This powerful symbol protects a person, or things, against the destructive forces of the devilmen. In those days, very few Tibetans would sleep in a house unless there was the sign of *obo* over the entrance.

Do you believe in such things as devils and demons?

DOC ANDERSON: There is a very strong belief in demons in many areas of the world. I am an old man, buddy, but I've seen many things that defy a logical, scientific explanation. There is a Prince of Darkness. There are legions of demonic entities who obtain special delight in tempting men. We have erred by dismissing the devil and his legions as superstition and folklore. He has grown stronger because we haven't watched for his treacherous deeds.

Can you perform the rites of exorcism to remove hexes and demonic possession?

DOC ANDERSON: Demonology is an ancient science and I've learned many rituals during my travels around the world. This is a serious matter and, as you know, special rites of exorcism are performed by certain priests of the Catholic church. I believe a person's life can absolutely be hexed. I believe our minds and bodies can be invaded by evil entities.

Do you believe these demons come from the hollow earth?

DOC ANDERSON: Demons are members of both the physical and invisible worlds. They dwell where they choose. According to my Tibetan friends, they can be spiritual or physical or they project themselves in various forms. Now, buddy, before you ask about the rites of getting rid of demons, let me say that I never give out this information. Such things should not be dabbled in for amusement. It is easy to make a mistake and conjure up the wrong entity.

Then, do you believe in a hollow earth?

DOC ANDERSON: Buddy, the world holds many secrets. Whether the hollow earth civilization is in the interior of this earth is another matter. It might be in another dimension of time and space. I could go into a trance state and bring back the truth about the subject. But, I think we should leave a few mysteries for our children. Someday, though, I am going to enter a trance state and find out about those pyramids at Shensi. Let's leave the subterranean world with the question of: Is it fact? Or is it fiction?

SUBTERRANEAN TUNNELS AND TREASURE VAULTS

A network of subterranean tunnels that link the continents of the world is one of the most persistent beliefs in hollow earth lore. Stories of these tunnels can be gleaned from the legends, folklore, and myths of almost every country. Monasteries on the craggy slopes of Tibet are supposed to be constructed over large, tranquil subterranean lakes. Many European visitors to Tibet have fascinated their western audiences with descriptions of tunnels that run from the monastery to the lake, then on down into the inner earth.

Several writers and explorers, notably those who ventured into Tibet during the early years of Oriental exploration, have reported on these underground tunnels. Ferdinald Ossendowski, a refugee from the Marxist revolutionists who overthrew the Czar's regime and brought Communism to Russia, was intrigued by the Far Eastern legends of the tunnels.

In his book, *Beasts, Men and Gods* (Edward Arnold, London, 1923) Ossendowski linked the Tibetan tunnels to the Oriental theology of a legendary King of the World. During his travels through the Orient, Ossendowski heard many legends of the believe-it-or-not type. However, he presented these stories to his readers in the belief that it would be unwise to dismiss all myths as pure fantasy.

The most intriguing story concerned a holy lama of Tibet who believed in the reality of a subterranean paradise. Embarking on a pilgrimage to discover this enchanted land, the lama eventually encountered a fisherman on the coast of Siam.

'It is the will of the gods that you sail with me,' declared the fisherman. 'I am an ambassador from land which you seek.'

'Can you provide proof?' inquired the wise man.

'I come from a land where people have two tongues,' replied the fisherman. 'My people can speak different languages with either tongue at the same time. The world from which I come is shunned by sailors. Few men may go there and return because all men boast of their adventures. However, you may sail with me to a small island and meet my companions who have come up from our subterranean kingdom.'

'Is this island nearby?' asked the lama.

'It is in the midst of the China Sea,' said the fisherman. 'There is no fee for the journey. I shall return you to these shores within a week.'

Whatever his reasons, curiosity, theological beliefs, or a natural yearning for adventure, the lama agreed to accompany the fisherman to the mysterious island. Upon his arrival on a rock and coral-studded isle, the lama was introduced to several tall, robed men who claimed to be from the subterranean world.

These strange beings led the old pilgrim to a bird cage. 'I saw a bird with sharp, fang-like teeth,' related the holy man. 'It was a species unknown to the surface world. I was also shown a strange animal with sixteen feet and one eye, like the legendary Cyclops of ancient times. The people assembled there told me they were from the subterranean kingdom of Agharta. They journeyed from the inner land in vehicles of a design unknown to surface men. They said their cars could be driven through subterranean tunnels that connected with all points of the earth.'

Did the old Tibetan holy man invent an imaginative story to intrigue a Western adventurer? Can we arbitrarily dismiss the account as fantasy? Many occultists believe that Eastern mystics have knowledge of secrets unknown to our present world, claiming there is seldom smoke without fire, and many legends have a basis in fact. The reader must determine his own attitude toward these unique facets of the hollow earth mystery.

There is an ancient legend among the Hindus of India that tells of a civilization of immense beauty beneath central Asia. Several underground cities are said to be located north of the Himalaya mountains, possibly in Afghanistan, or under the Hindu Kush. This subterranean Shangri-la is inhabited by a race of golden people who seldom communicate with the surface world. From time to time, they travel into outer land through tunnels that stretch upward in many directions. Entrances to the tunnels are believed to be hidden in several of the ancient cities of the Orient. Tunnel entrances are said to be in Ellore and the Ajunta caverns in the Chandore Mountain range of India.

'The lamas were very convincing about the tunnels,' said R. C. 'Doc' Anderson, the Rossville, Georgia, psychic. 'The Tibetan holy men frequently told me there were vast caves beneath North, South, and Central America. They said these caves were connected through tunnels to the surface world. Underground cities are supposed to be built in these vast cavities inside the earth. These cavern people are an ancient race, possibly the Atlanteans. The lamas asserted that these secret tunnels and cavern cities are illuminated by an unusual green light which is favorable to crops, long life, and good health.'

Tibetans also told Doc Anderson that Atlantis, the legendary continent, had a network of tunnels and passages extending beneath the ocean in many directions. 'The tunnels were used by the merchants of Atlantis to carry on their trade with other countries,' said Doc Anderson. 'The lamas showed me a map of the underground passages leading from a large island in the Atlantic ocean to Europe, Africa, South America, and America. I was informed that this map was extremely old and that no other white man had ever seen it.'

A similar legend of subterranean tunnels of ancient construction, and an unknown origin, was brought to the attention of early explorers in Martinique, in the West Indies. In his reports on his explorations, Columbus revealed the West Indies claimed the island was once the site of many vast cities. 'These ancient communities were connected by tunnels that ran beneath the earth,' a West Indian informed Columbus. 'Our land was once ruled by giant women warriors. They fought with a tribe of cannibals. Whenever the cannibal men attacked, the women rushed down through the great tunnels. If their enemies stormed the tunnels, the women killed them with arrows from their giant bows.'

In his book, *Mysteries of Ancient South America* (the Citadel Press, New York, 1956), author Harold T. Wilkins related that in March 1942, a Mr. and Mrs. Lamb (no other identification) from California, were personal guests of President Franklin D. Roosevelt at the White House. The couple had reportedly discovered a tribe of uncivilized Indians in the Mexican state of Chiappas. These Indians, possibly members of the Lancandones tribe, said they guarded an ancient, unknown Mayan city. The Lambs informed President Roosevelt the old city included a temple with a subterranean vault. Inside the vault were gold plates, enscribed with a record of man's history on earth. They also declared the gold plates had predicted the outbreak of World War II.

'The Lambs told the President that the gold sheets recorded history back beyond the great flood,' reported Gunther Rosenberg. 'The Indian tribesmen seldom visited the secret city, except to worship. Then they held ritualistic ceremonies in the Mayan temple and worshipped their ancient gods of the underworld.'

'This may be the same lost city mentioned by Abbe Charles Etienne Brasseur-de-Bourbourg, the scholarly, religious administrator of Chiappas, Mexico, in the early 1850s. The Abbe recorded his experiences in a journal, mentioning rumors of a lost city along the edges of the Mexican frontier. He said that people from this hidden city frequently appeared in the pueblos and towns to barter for supplies. They vanished as quickly as they appeared when they were questioned about their origin.'

A Spanish priest, assigned to a parish in Guatemala in the late 16th century, wrote a detailed history of that country. Fuentes told of lost cities, ancient and unknown tribes of degenerate Indians, and amazing subterranean tunnels that linked these ancient pueblos. Fuentes wrote:

> The amazing structure of the tunnels of the pueblo of Pucheta has been of interest to all. The tunnel is made of firm, solid cement. It runs beneath the earth and through the interior of the land for a distance of nine leagues. This *subterranea* is substantial proof of the power of the ancient kings and their subjects who once ruled in this land.

Fuentes was unable to discover why these long tunnels were constructed by the ancients. The tunnels would be more than thirty miles long if they were measured on the basis of the old Castilian league. Do these tunnels in Guatemala have a secret entrance to the great subterranean tunnels beneath the earth? Did this unknown race use the tunnels as a method of defense, hiding in these holes whenever danger appeared? It is evident that the men who lived in these enigmatic lands many years ago knew more than we are willing to admit.

J. Lloyd Stephens, an adventurer, traveler and a friend of Madame Blavatsky, was exploring the areas of western Guatemala in 1838–39. Later, in both London and New York, Stephens astonished newsmen with stories of unusual ruins near the pueblo of Chajol. Stephens said:

> There are ruins beyond Santa Cruz del Quinche that are unknown to our explorers. I was traveling with a band of native Indians near the headwaters of the Rio Usumacinta. After many days of hard travel, we climbed to the summit of a large ridge along the Sierra Cordillera. At a

height of 10,000 feet I could look over an immense plain that extended to the south and down into the Gulf of Mexico. From that vantage point I saw a marvelous city that extended over a great area. There were high, white turrets that glistened in the sun.

Stephens motioned for his porters to march toward the city. 'I was extremely excited at the thought of finding a lost metropolis in this dense green jungle,' he said later.

'This is as far as a white man may go,' an elderly Indian informed Stephens. 'The people in that city know that white invaders have conquered this land. They murder any white man who enters the city.'

'How have they remained undiscovered for so many years?' asked Stephens.

'They have no coins, no livestock, or domestic animals,' said the old Indian. 'The buildings you see are not inhabited. They have left the city and moved underground to save themselves from the white invaders.'

'How do they live underground?' inquired Lloyd Stephens. 'Without sunlight, they would surely die after a few weeks in a cave.'

The old Indian looked at the explorer with amusement. 'There are many secrets in this world,' he said. 'These people have known the formula for the great light for thousands of years.'

'What great light?'

The Indian pointed to the earth and up into the cloudy sky. 'The great light is the secret of all things,' he said. 'It was given to these people many ages ago by the gods from beneath the earth.'

Stephens argued with his Indian packers, but he was unable to convince them to enter the city. Frustrated, his curiosity at a fevered pitch, Lloyd Stephens reluctantly followed his guides down the Rio Usumacinta river. As he left the tortuous, hilly jungles of western Guatemala Stephens wondered how many ancient races lived beneath the earth. These abandoned cities had once hummed with life. Now, he wondered if Cortez and his Conquistadors had seized the real treasure from the sallow-faced Aztec priests. Was the great light the real bonanza?

Many occultists and treasure hunters fervently believe that the world's greatest storehouse of riches moulders in a subterranean South American tunnel. In the 15th century, when Francisco Pizarro and his brutal Spanish Conquistadors invaded South America, they destroyed the Incan civilization. Their murderous atrocities, extreme cruelties, and rapacious lust for gold and women, virtually eliminated the entire Incan empirc. The last hopes of the gentle Incans were slashed to pieces by Toledo steel. Yet, not all of the Conquistadors were intent on loot. Don Mancio Serra de Leguisamo was stationed in Cuzco, Peru, in September, 1589. He wrote of the changes that the Conquistadors had brought to these ancient people:

> The Incan Peruvians were so free from crime and excesses, the men as well as the women, that the Indian who had 100,000 pesos of gold in his home left the door open and unlocked. He simply placed a small stick across the door as a sign that he was out. No one would enter or take anything that was inside while he was gone... When the Incans discovered that we put locks, keys, and guards on our doors they believed it was because of fear of them, that they might not kill us. They could not believe that anyone would steal the property of another person. So, when they learned that we had thieves among us, and men who tried to make their daughters commit sin, they despised us. Things have now come to pass, owing to the bad example we have set for them, that the natives have changed into people who no longer do good. They are as evil as ourselves. I hope to do what I can to discharge my conscience.

Most occultists believe that a golden horde of Incan

treasure, artifacts, and precious stones are hidden in a subterranean tunnel in South America. While the Spanish Conquistadors were looting the empire, an enormous amount of Incan riches vanished. Since then, thousands of gold-hungry prospectors and mystical adventurers have searched for this elusive loot. There are few clues to the treasure's site.

Those who believe in the hollow earth theory declare that the Incans took a large number of their people, and most of their treasure, into a gigantic tunnel that led down into the inner-earth.

'There were more than 10 million Incans when the Spaniards first invaded their land,' reported Gunther Rosenberg. 'In 1571, only forty years after the first white man arrived in Peru, nine million Incans had died or vanished.'

As far back as A.D. 1545, Pedro Cieza de Deleon said that every ship in the world would be unable to carry the riches of the Incan empire to the Spanish king's storehouses in Seville, Spain. 'If all the gold that is hidden in Peru . . . was collected, it would be impossible for the world to coin it,' said the Spaniard. 'The quantity is tremendous and yet despite our best efforts, we got very little of what existed. Indians have told me that the treasure is so well hidden that even they do not know the hiding place.'

During a visit to South America recently, I inspected a wrinkled, yellowed parchment in the archives at Cuzco, Peru. It was written many years ago by Felipe de Pomares, who claimed there was a rich Incan treasure sealed in a tunnel beneath the ancient fortress at Cuzco. Even today, Peruvians claimed there is a secret society composed of Indians, and a few selected white men, who guard the treasure. The parchment at Cuzco tells of a Carlos Inca, the descendent of the last Incan emperor. He had married a Spanish woman, Dona Maria Esquidel, a fiery beauty. Her sharp tongue and shrill voice slashed throught the Incan's consciousness like a sword. 'You are no lord or hidaldo,' snapped Maria Esquidel. 'I married you expecting riches. Now my friends ridicule me because you are only a poverty-stricken Indian.'

Carlos blinked his eyes, then shrugged his shoulders. 'We do well raising our sheep. A man should not be too ambitious.'

'I am tired of the smell of sheep,' shouted Maria, shrilly. 'Everyone talks of the gold that is hidden in this land. If you are the son of a king, you must know where the treasure lies.'

Carlos tried not to argue with his wife. Although he was the son of an Incan king, he was always a little afraid of the beautiful Spanish woman. In their marriage, it was Maria who was the ambitious realist. Carlos was the dreamer. Maria was the driving leader, and Carlos was her subject. As time passed, Maria's mind manifested a vivid picture of the Incan treasure. She was tired of the boring dullness, and isolated routine of life in Peru. She wanted to triumphantly return to Spain with her handsome Incan husband. The regal journey back to her homeland could only be accomplished if she had gold.

Day after day, Maria whined, wheedled, and argued with her husband. She confused him by making a sudden twist of her shoulders, then playing the role of a warm, loving wife. 'You know where the treasure lies,' she whispered huskily. 'Once I have seen the treasure, I shall be content to live here with you.'

Continually nagged by his wife, Carlos finally consented to show her the treasure. 'We must be certain that everyone is asleep,' he said. 'There are many men guarding the entrance. We risk death by entering the tunnel.'

After a lengthy walk from their hacienda, Carlos blindfolded his wife. He turned her around several times, and when she was disoriented, he led her into the tunnel. Later, Dona Maria said the tunnel entrance was near the old fortress at Cuzco.

After the blindfold was removed from her eyes, Dona Maria was led down a smooth stone stairway. The stairs stopped at a dusty, polished floor of a subterranean vault. 'The place was enormous in size. There were gold and silver ingots, precious jewels, and temple ornaments from the Incan empire,' Dona Maria said. 'Along the walls, as far as I could see, were giant gold statues of ancient Incan emperors. Carlos let me select an emerald jewel before we returned to the surface. I wanted the whole treasure.'

In the weeks that followed, the shrewish wife used shouts, screams, and her womanly wiles, to get more treasure from the subterranean vault. Carlos was unperturbed by her selfish actions. 'The treasure is there for all time,' he said. 'It belongs to those who come after us.'

After two years of marital discord, Carlos reentered the tunnel. He brought back a small bag of gold and handful of precious stones. He gave the treasure to his Spanish wife. 'Here is what you seek,' he said. 'Take this, return to your homeland, and never marry the son of a king again. He may want love rather than riches.'

Dona Maria left Cuzco, sailed on a galleon to Spain, and disappeared from the pages of occult history. The insect-bitten brittle parchment at Cuzco does not tell of the ultimate destiny of Carlos Inca. Before she sailed, the fiery Spanish beauty told her story to the authorities.

The mystery of the subterranean labyrinth and tunnels goes far back into the days of antiquity. Any initiate who might divulge the location of the entrances would do so under the possibility of death by his companions. About 1835, stories of the tunnel treasure excited the Peruvian authorities. 'They sent out several expedition to search for the concealed openings,' reported Gunther Rosenberg. 'For more than 20 years, the Peruvian government hunted for the tunnel. They were no wiser at the conclusion of their project than when they started.'

Madame Helene Petrovena Blavatsky, the noted Russian-American mystic and adventuress, traveled throughout South America for two years between 1848 and 1850. She became intrigued by the curious legends of subterranean tunnels and although the region was infested with bandits, she hoped to verify their existence.

She met an Italian soldier of fortune who said he had once visited the underground labyrinth. 'It defies the imagination. Words can't describe these great caves,' the adventurer told Madame Blavatsky. 'It is like stepping into the land of Aladdin. The old magicians and the Incan priests say the tunnels were there when their people first came to South America.'

Madame Blavatsky journeyed throughout Peru in pursuit of more data on the subterranean tunnels. She heard accounts from many different, entirely unconnected people. She said:

> We reached Arica, near sunset, and at a certain point on the lonely coast we were struck by the appearance of an enormous rock, nearly perpendicular, which stood in mournful solitude on that shore, and apart from the cordilliera of the Andes. As the last rays of the setting sun struck the rock, one can make out, with an ordinary opera-glass, curious hieroglyphics inscribed on the volcanic surface.
>
> When Cuzco was the capital of old Peru, it contained a temple of the sun famed far and near for its magnificence. It was roofed with thick plates of gold and its walls were covered with the same precious metal. The eaves troughs, carrying off the rainwater, were also made of pure gold. In the west wall, the architects had contrived an aperture in such a way that when the sunbeams reached it, it caught and focused them inside the temple's nave and sanctuary. Stretching inside the temple, like a golden chain, from one sparkling point to another, the rays encircled the walls, illuminating the grim idols, and disclosing certain mystic signs, at other times invisible.

Madame Blavatsky, and many others who believe in the tunnels, declared an entrance is near old Cuzco. 'It is masked beyond discovery,' Madame Blavatsky said. This entrance at Cuzco supposedly leads to an enormous underground passage that runs south for a distance of 380 miles. There, the tunnel rolls under Bolivia for another 900 miles. In Bolivia, occultists claim the tunnel connects with the intercontinental labyrinths of the underpeople.

'Legends say the South American passage contains a royal tomb,' said Albert McDonald, president of the Hollow Earth Society. 'Whoever constructed these interior highways were ingenious people. Like the architects and engineers of old Egypt, they set up elaborate devices to trap anyone who tried to rob the tomb. The Incans developed hidden doors of carved stones. These massive slabs are pivoted to close so tight that there is no sign of a crack or joint. The royal mausoleum can be found only by interpreting the symbols that are inscribed on the walls of the tunnels.'

These pivoting stone slabs conceal the openings that lead into the tunnels. The southern end of the tunnel is located in the stark, desolate salt desert of Atacama, according to occultists. This is a waterless wasteland, shrouded by leaden skies, and whipped by harsh desert winds. If a tunnel entrance does exist somewhere in the *desierto de atacama*, it would be hidden by swirling sands. Few men have ventured into that harsh terrain in search of an elusive, pivoting stone door.

Nearly a hundred years ago, Madame Blavatsky said she possessed a map of these fantastic tunnels. 'It was an accurate plan of the tunnel, the sepulchre, the great treasure chamber and the hidden, pivoted rock doors,' she said. 'It was given to us by an old Peruvian; but if we had ever thought of profiting from the secret, it would have required the cooperation of the Peruvian and Bolivian governments on an extensive scale. To say nothing of physical obstacles, no one individual or small party could undertake such an exploration without encountering the army of brigands and smugglers with which the coast is infested, and which, in fact, includes nearly the entire population. The mere task of purifying the mephitic air of a tunnel not entered for centuries would also be a serious one. There the treasure lies, and tradition says it will lie till the last vestige of Spanish rule disappears from the whole of North and South America.'

The central plateau of Brazil, known as the Mato Grosso, is one of the most mysterious, unexplored regions in the world. Along the headwaters of the Amazon river, there are vast stretches of dense jungle that have never been seen by white men. Savage tribes of Indians inhabit these lands and their poison-tipped arrows remain effective in this modern age. The few explorers who have attempted to penetrate the Mato Grosso often waste away from jungle fever or rare tropical diseases. They are open prey for both Indians and the beasts of the jungles.

Stories about the Mato Grosso are as wild as the land and its inhabitants.

'. . . There are cities of gold inside the jungle,' some claim. 'These are the ruins of the Atlantean civilization.'

'. . . Prehistoric beasts still roam the swamps,' others declare.

'. . . There are underground cities, entrances to the tunnels, and marvels of the ages hidden there,' hollow earth theorists proclaim.

Admittedly, there may be lost cities, uncharted lakes, and 'white Indians' within the interior of the Brazilian jungle. One explorer claimed to have absolute proof of a fabulous city of gold, possibly located beneath a mountain or under a lake.

The explorer was Colonel Percy Fawcett, who plunged into the jungles in 1925, accompanied by his son, Jack, and Raleigh Rimell, another Englishman. They never returned from their quest for the legendary city. Hollow earth believers claim they found the lost city and they're still there after forty-five years.

Fawcett wrote that he knew where there were ancient ruins of large cities in the jungles. 'These amazing ruins of ancient cities are incomparably older than those in Egypt,' he declared.

The Englishman became intrigued by the legendary ruins

in Brazil after he discovered a historical document in the archives at Rio de Janeiro. A Portuguese expedition entered the Mato Grosso in 1734, seeking gold and silver. 'They were in the midst of the central plateau when they came upon a large mountain range,' said an authority on Fawcett's disappearance. 'They noticed a small fissure, or crack, in one of the mountains. They crawled through it and discovered an enormous city. The buildings appeared to have been devastated by an earthquake with huge blocks of granite torn from the buildings and strewn about. The document tells of a sacrificial altar carved from solid gold, hieroglyphics, and strange faces carved into stone. Gold coins were scattered about the ruins and there were several underground shafts on the edge of the deserted city.

The manuscript, No. 512, can be obtained on microfilm for $2 (cashier's check) from Biblioteca Nationale, Rio de Janeiro. 'It reveals the Portuguese knew they had discovered a lost civilization,' said the authority. 'As they prepared to rush back to civilization, they encountered two men among the ruins. These beings had white skin, long black hair, and they wore robes.'

Before the gold-hunters reached Rio de Janeiro, they sent a native runner ahead with a written report of their incredible discovery. 'The runner arrived on the coast without any problems,' the Brazilian continued. 'The report was given to the authorities and everyone waited anxiously for the expedition to come down river. They simply vanished! They were never heard of again. We don't know if they decided to return to the city, or if they were killed by the Indians. Or, did the white men in robes murder them to keep the location of the city a secret?'

In the past two centuries, many expeditions sought the lost city. In the early years of this century, the Krupps of Essen, Germany, armament makers for Germany's military machine, financed a search with a $400,000 grant. It was one of the best-equipped expeditions to ever start into the Brazilian jungle. At night, the savage Indians attacked the group with poisoned darts and arrows. By day, the Germans were disturbed by the constant roar of jungle drums. Some Indians of the Mato Grosso were cannibals and head-hunters. 'They can see better in the dark than a cat,' said one participant. 'The Krupp expedition managed to overcome those problems. Yet, it was just so large that we couldn't maintain a supply line. We had to turn back when our food ran out.'

Harold T. Wilkins, and other authors, have mentioned an expedition into the jungles in 1927 that may have reached the 'city under the mountain.' A report from a Senor Medellin related that '. . . here we ambushed and caught a dwarfish man, about four feet tall, with very red eyes. He had a thick bushy beard. The beard reached down to his waist. His arms were muscular, yet rather fat and big. He wore an unusual leather belt around his waist, with a buckle made from solid gold. We were to meet more of these pygmy people later and they had a dark-colored white skin.'

The most unusual feature of the pygmies were their eyes. 'They had red eyes that were cat-like in appearance,' said Senor Medellin. 'Their eyes shined like a cat in the firelight.'

In *Mysteries of Ancient South America,* Wilkins quoted his informant as saying the 'dwarfs lived in tunnels on the outskirts of the city, or rooms in the rock . . . (and) carried a long curved knife of pure gold!'

Apparently, the Medellin expedition left the 'city beneath the mountain' with as much gold as they could carry. Brazilians often tell of other men who have found the city, and profited by lugging a fortune in gold from the ruins.

Colonel Fawcett felt the lost city was incredibly old, quite important, and a possible clue to the Atlantis legend. Fawcett had served with the British Royal Artillery and, during a stretch in India, he became deeply interested in Buddhism and mysticism.

As Fawcett, his son, Jack, and Rimell pushed further into the Brazilian jungle, they telegraphed a final message to London. '. . . If there is any attempt to send an expedition after us, to discover our fate or fortune – and we expect to be away for two or three years – for God's sake, stop them!' Fawcett cabled.

He also said that the 'city of gold' was guarded by a ferocious tribe of short, squat cannibals. 'Fawcett said they lived in holes and caves along the outer edges of the city,' explained a Brazilian authority. 'They were very dangerous, although they were armed only with rocks and clubs.'

Col. Fawcett had been into the Brazilian interior on previous expeditions and, in May, 1910, he lectured before the Royal Geographical Society in London. His audience was astonished to learn of the Morcegos, a bat-like race that sleeps by day in a great hole in the ground. 'They cover their holes with a wickerwork lid,' Col. Fawcett said. 'They sleep throughout the day and they emerge from their subterranean holes at night to hunt and prowl. They have tremendously keen eyesight and a heightened sense of smell.'

Albert McDonald and the Hollow Earth Society believe Col. Fawcett and his companions reached the lost city, found a tunnel leading into the inner earth, and vanished into the inner land. 'Nine years after her husband disappeared, Mrs. Nina Fawcett received telepathic messages from him,' McDonald said. 'She always felt her husband was alive, possibly held as a prisoner to maintain the secret of the lost city.'

Ray Levin, a treasure hunter, has spent several months searching for lost cities, tunnel entrances, and buried treasure in South America. Levin wrote recently:

> Down here a lot of people believe that Colonel Fawcett was not searching for a dead city. He was looking for a subterranean city that is inhabited by the survivors of Atlantis. There is said to be a tunnel entrance somewhere in the Roncador mountains and the shaft leads down into a subterranean metropolis. I'm learning some of the Indian dialects and I've been told that once you enter the tunnels, you are not allowed to leave. Which would be one way to explain Fawcett's disappearance. He found

the city, that fabled golden proof of Atlantis, but he was not allowed to return to tell his story.

I've been very careful in my search for the golden goodies down here. There are still bandits in the back country and a revolutionary group has formed here in the past few years. Also, *Der Spider* is down here, a Nazi group set up to aid Hitler's cohorts to their escape after the Third Reich fell. A wandering Jew like me can't be too careful.

An old man told me that there was a number of immigrants, who helped in the revolution led by General Isidro Lopez, took off into the Roncador mountains. They simply vanished and he swore they went to live in the subterranean cities.

I rented an airplane last month and flew over a couple of likely sites. Now, I understand why the Mato Grosso remains a mystery. In some places, the fog never lifts, and in others, the stuff doesn't clear off until late afternoon.

Do I believe in the tunnels and the treasure?

As far back as Cortez and his *conquistadores*, we've heard stories about the fabled cities of gold. I believe these cities exist, perhaps not on the surface world, but down below in the interior. There are dozens of maps down here, most of them worthless, but each one should be checked out. I have obtained the old Portuguese document left by the gold-hunters. There may be something about directions or routes that everyone has missed.

Tunnels . . . lost Incan treasure . . . Lost worlds and cities of gold in the Brazilian jungles. Whether it is true or false, the legends of the hollow earth contain the essential ingredients of exciting adventure.

THE COMING RACE AND VRIL POWER

A macabre area of the hollow earth mystery was a Nazi-oriented secret occult society in Germany before, and during Hitler's reign as dictator. This society of initiates was based on Bulwer Lytton's novel, *The Coming Race* (Wm. Blackwood and Son, Edinburgh). *The Coming Race* is out of print; copies cost $80.00 to $100.00 from rare book dealers. Lytton is best known throughout the world for his popular novel, *The Last Days of Pompeii.*

The Coming Race tells of advanced beings who live in the interior of the earth; they have powers far advanced above surface *homo sapiens*. In time, they plan to emerge and conquer the surface world. 'The Nazis established the *Luminous Lodge of the Vril Society*,' reported Gunther Rosenberg, of the European Occult Research Society. 'Lytton described a vril as a form of energy. The *Vril Society* was associated with other occult groups in Germany during the Third Reich. They believed that the Lords of the Universe lived in the center of the earth. Men on the surface must become God-like and make an alliance with the inner race. Otherwise, we will be enslaved to build the New Cities for the Coming Race.'

Although it is an occult classic, Bulwer Lytton's *The Coming Race* is rarely found outside academic libraries. Even then, it is usually a carefully guarded volume in rare book rooms.

'I am a native of ——, in the United States of America. My ancestors migrated from England in the reign of Charles II; and my grandfather was not undistinguished in the War of Independence,' is the way Bulwer Lytton started *The Coming Race*.

At age sixteen, the anonymous narrator was sent to England for his education. After his father died when he was twenty-one, he was 'left well off, and having a taste for travel and adventure, I resigned, for a time, all pursuit of the almighty dollar, and became a desultory wanderer over the face of the earth.

'In the year 18—, happening to be in ——, I was invited by a professional engineer, with whom I had made my acquaintance, to visit the recesses of the —— mine, upon which he was employed.

> Let me say then, as briefly as possible, that I accompanied the engineer to the interior of the mine, and became so strangely fascinated by its gloomy wonders, and so interested in my friend's explorations, that I prolonged my stay in the neighborhood, and descended daily, for some weeks, into the vaults and gallieries hollowed by nature and art beneath the surface of the earth. The engineer was persuaded that a far richer deposit of mineral wealth than had been detected would be found in a new shaft that had been commenced under his operation. In piercing this shaft, we came one day upon a chasm jagged and seemingly charred at the sides, as if burst asunder at some distant period by volcanic fires. Down this chasm my friend caused himself to be lowered in a 'cage,' having first tested the atmosphere by safety lamp. He remained nearly an hour in the abyss. When he returned he was pale and with an anxious expression of face, very different from its ordinary character, which was open and cheerful.

After a time, the narrator succeeded in getting the engineer to relate his experiences in the shaft. 'I will tell you all,' said the engineer, sipping from a flask of brandy. 'When the cage stopped, I was on a ridge of rock and below me was the chasm, slanting down to a considerable depth. At the bottom of it to my surprise, streamed upward a steady, brilliant light.

'Could it have been volcanic fire?' asked the young man.

'In that case I would have felt the heat,' replied the

engineer. 'Still, for everyone's safety, I wanted to clear it up. I could venture down along the shaft and I clambered out of the cage and, as I drew nearer to the light, the chasm became wider, and at last, I saw to my unspeakable amazement, a broad level road at the bottom of the abyss, illuminated as far as the eye could see by what seemed artificial gas lamps placed at regular intervals, as in the city. I heard confusedly at a distance a hum as of human voices. I know, of course, that no rival miners are at work in this district. Whose could be these voices? What human hands could have leveled that road and marshalled those lamps?'

The engineer and his young friend vowed to descend into the mine shaft and solve the mystery. They knew there was a superstitious belief among miners that gnomes and fiends dwelled in the bowels of the earth. Lowered by the cage, the two men then climbed down the precarious shaft.

'He had exaggerated nothing,' the narrator said. 'I heard the sounds he had heard – a mingled indescribable hum as of voices and a dull tramp as of feet. Straining my eyes farther down, I clearly beheld at a distance the outline of some large building. It could not be mere natural rock, it was too symmetrical, with huge heavy Egyptian-like columns, and the whole lighted as from within. I had with me a small pocket telescope, and by the aid of this I could distinguish, near the buildings I mention, two forms which seemed human . . .'

During their final descent into the strange land below them, the men slipped and fell a considerable distance. 'When I recovered my senses I saw my companion an inanimate mass before me,' the hero wrote. 'Life was utterly extinct. While I was bending over his corpse in grief and horror, I heard close at hand a strange sound between a snort and a hiss; and turning instinctively to the quarter from which it came, I saw emerging from a small fissure in the rock a vast and terrible head, with open jaws and dull, ghastly, hungry eyes – the head of a monstrous reptile resembling that of a crocodile or alligator, but infintely larger than the largest creature of that kind I had ever beheld in my travels.'

The young man fled to safety 'at utmost speed. I stopped at last, ashamed of my panic, and returned to the spot where I had left the body of my friend. It was gone; doubtless the monster had already drawn it into its den and devoured it.'

Ropes, grappling hooks, and other equipment had vanished. 'I was alone in this strange world amidst the bowels of the earth,' he said, mournfully.

Later, when he walked into the city, Bulwer Lytton's narrator noticed that the architecture was

> more ornamental and more fantastically graceful than Egyptian architecture allows . . . and now there came out of this building a form – human; was it human? It stood on the broad way and looked around, beheld me and approached. It came within a few yards of me, and at the sight and presence of it an indescribable awe and tremor seized me, rooting my feet to the ground. It reminded me of the symbolical images of Genius or Demon that are seen on Etruscan vases or limned on the walls of Eastern sepulchres – images that borrow the outlines of man, and are yet of another race. It was tall, not gigantic, but tall as the tallest men below the height of giants.
>
> Its chief covering seemed to me to be composed of large wings folded over its breast and reaching down to its knees; the rest of its attire was composed of an under tunic and leggings of some thin fiberous material. It wore on its head a kind of tiara that shone with jewels and carried in its right hand a slender staff of bright metal like polished steel.
>
> But the face! It was that which inspired my awe and my terror. It was the face of a man, but yet of a type of man distinct from our own extant races. The nearest approach to it in outline and expression is the face of the sculptured sphinx – so regular in its calm, intellectual,

mysterious beauty. Its color was peculiar, more like that of the red man than any other variety of our species, and yet different from it – a richer and softer hue, with large black eyes, deep and brilliant, and brows arched as a semicircle. The face was beardless; but a nameless something in the aspect, tranquil though the expression, roused that instinct of danger which the sight of a tiger or serpent arouses. I felt that this manlike image was endowed with forces inimical to man. As it drew near, a cold shudder came over me. I fell on my knees and covered my face with my hands.

Later, the astonished young man discovered the wings were mechanical objects operated by Vril power. The people who inhabited the cavern world were known as the Vril-ya. The narrator became a guest of a powerful Vril-ya and his daughter, Zee. During an inner earth ritual, he was shocked by Vril power. Bulwer Lytton wrote:

The view beyond was of a wild and solemn beauty impossible to describe, – the vast ranges of precipitous rock which formed the distant background, the intermediate valleys of mystic many-colored herbage, the flash of waters, many of them like streams of roseate flame, the serene lustre diffused over all by myriads of lamps, combined to form a whole of which no words of mine can convey adequate description; so splendid was it, yet so sombre; so lovely, yet so awful.

But my attention was soon diverted from these nether landscapes. Suddenly there arose, as from the streets below, a burst of joyous music; then a winged form soared into the space; another, as in chase of the first, another and another; others after others, till the crowd grew thick and the number countless. But how describe the fantastic grace of these forms in their undulating movements! They appeared engaged in some sport or amusement; now forming into opposite squadrons; now scattering; now each group threading the other, soaring, descending, interweaving, severing; all in measured time to the music below, as if in the dance of the fabled Peri.

I turned my gaze on my host in a feverish wonder. I ventured to place my hand on the large wings that lay folded on his breast, and in doing so a slight shock as of electricity passed through me. I recoiled in fear; my host smiled, and, as if courteously to gratify my curiosity, slowly expanded his pinions. I observed that his garment beneath then became dilated as a bladder that fills with air.

The arms seemed to slide into the wings, and in another moment he had launched himself into the luminous atmosphere, and hovered there, still, and with outspread wings, as an eagle that basks in the sun. Then, rapidly as an eagle swoops, he rushed downwards into the midst of one of the groups, skimming through the midst, and as suddenly again soaring aloft.

Thereon, three forms, in one of which I thought to recognize my host's daughter, detached themselves from the rest, and followed him as a bird sportively follows a bird. My eyes dazzled with the lights and bewildered by the throngs, ceased to distinguish the gyrations and evolutions of these winged playmates, till presently my host re-emerged from the crowd and alighted at my side.

The strangeness of all I had seen began now to operate fast on my senses; my mind itself began to wander. Though not inclined to be superstitious, nor hitherto believing that man could be brought into bodily communication with demons, I felt the terror and the wild excitement with which, in the Gothic ages, a traveller might have persuaded himself that he witnessed a *sabbat* of fiends and witches.

I have a vague recollection of having attempted with vehement gesticulation, and forms of exorcism, and loud incoherent words, to repel my courteous and indulgent host; of his mild endeavours to calm and soothe me; of his intelligent conjecture that my fright and bewilderment were occasioned by the difference of form and movement between us which the wings that had excited my marvelling curiosity had, in exercise, made still more strongly perceptible; of the gentle smile with which he had sought to dispel my alarm by dropping the wings to the ground and endeavouring to show me that they were but a mechanical contrivance.

That sudden transformation did but increase my horror, and as extreme fright often shows itself by extreme daring, I sprang at his throat like a wild beast. On an instant I was felled to the ground as by an electric shock, and the last confused images floating before my sight ere I became wholly insensible, were the form of my host kneeling beside me with one hand on my forehead, and the beautiful calm face of his daughter, with large, deep, inscrutable eyes intently fixed upon my own.

The young man was in the hospital for several days suffering from his nervousness and the after-shock from vril. After his recovery and subsequent release from the hospital, our hero is intrigued by the vril force.

'What is vril?' I asked.

Therewith Zee began to enter into an explanation of which I understood very little, for there is no word in any language I know which is an exact synonym for vril. I should call it electricity, except that it comprehends in its manifold branches other forces of nature, to which, in our scientific nomenclature, differing names are assigned, such as magnetism, galvanism, etc. These people consider that in vril they have arrived at the unity in natural energic agencies, which has been conjectured by many philosophers above ground, and which Faraday thus intimates under the more cautious term of correlation:

'I have long held an opinion,' says the illustrious experimentalist, 'almost amounting to a conviction, in common,

I believe, with many other lovers of natural knowledge, that the various forms under which the forces of matter are made manifest have one common origin; or, in other words, are so directly related and mutually dependent, that they are convertible, as it were, into one another, and possess equivalents of power in their action.'

These subterranean philosophers assert that by one operation of vril, which Faraday would perhaps call 'atmospheric magnetism,' they can influence the variations of temperature – in plain words, the weather; that by other operations, akin to those ascribed to mesmerism, electrobiology, odic force, etc., but applied scientifically through vril conductors, they can exercise influence over minds, and bodies animal and vegetable, to an extent not surpassed in the romances of our mystics. To all such agencies they give the common name of vril.

Zee asked me if in my world, it was not known that all the faculties of the mind could be quickened to a degree unknown in the waking state, by trance or vision, in which the thoughts of one brain could be transmitted to another, and knowledge be thus rapidly interchanged. I replied that there were amongst us stories told of such trance or vision, and that I had heard much and seen something of the mode in which they were artificially effected, as in mesmeric clairvoyance; but that these practices had fallen much into disuse or contempt, partly because of the gross impostures to which they had been made subservient, and partly because, even where the effects upon certain abnormal constitutions were genuinely produced, the effects, when fairly examined and analysed, were very unsatisfactory – not to be relied upon for any systematic truthfulness or any practical purpose, and rendered very mischievous to credulous persons by the superstitions they tended to produce.

Zee received my answers with much benignant attention, and said that similar instances of abuse and credulity had been familiar to their own scientific experience in the infancy of their knowledge, and while the properties of vril were misapprehended, but that she reserved further discussion on this subject till I was more fitted to enter into it. She contented herself with adding, that it was through the agency of vril, while I had been placed in the state of trance, that I had been made acquainted with the rudiments of their language.

I was never allowed to handle the vril staff for fear of some terrible accident occasioned by my ignorance of its use; and I have no doubt that it requires much skill and practice in the exercise of its various powers. It is hollow, and has in the handle several stops, keys, or springs by which its force can be altered, modified, or directed – so that by one process it destroys, by another it heals – by one it can rend the rock, by another disperse the vapour – by one it affects bodies, by another it can exercise a certain influence over minds. It is usually carried in the convenient size of a walking-staff, but it has slides by which it can be lengthened or shortened at will. When used for special purposes, the upper part rests in the hollow of the palm with the fore and middle fingers protruded.

I was assured, however, that its power was not equal in all, but proportioned to the amount of certain vril properties in the wearer in affinity, or rapport with the purposes to be affected. Some were more potent to destroy, others to heal, etc.; much also depended on the calm and steadiness of volition in the manipulator. They assert that the full exercise of vril power can only be acquired by constitutional temperament – i.e., by hereditarily transmitted organisation – and that a female infant of four years old belonging to the Vril-ya races can accomplish feats with the wand placed for the first time in her hand, which a life spent in its practice would not enable the strongest and most skilled mechanician, born out of the pale of the Vril-ya,to achieve. All these wands are not equally complicated; those intrusted to children are much simpler than those born by sages of either sex, and constructed with a view to the special object in which the children are employed; which, as I have before said, is among the youngest children the most destructive. In the wands of wives and mothers the correlative destroying force is usually abstracted, the healing power fully charged. I wish I could say more in detail of this singular conductor of the vril fluid, but its machinery is as exquisite as its effects are marvelous.

I should say, however, that this people have invented certain tubes by which the vril fluid can be conducted towards the object it is meant to destroy, throughout a distance almost indefinite; at least I put it modestly when I say from 500 to 600 miles. And their mathematical science as applied to such purpose is so nicely accurate, that on the report of some observer in an air-boat, any member of the vril department can estimate unerringly the nature of intervening obstacles, the height to which the projectile instrument should be raised, and the extent to which it should be charged, so as to reduce to ashes within a space of time too short for me to venture to specify it, a capital twice as vast as London.

GENESIS OF THE VRIL-YA

Eventually, the narrator of Bulwer Lytton's *The Coming Race* escaped from the cavern world of the Vril-ya, aided by a young cavern woman who flew him back up the shaft and into the mine. Lytton, who was a member of several secret societies, said the manuscript was fiction. However, German Nazis, especially members of the *Luminous Lodge of the Vril Society,* fervently believed that Lytton's book was, in reality, based on fact. Mystical members of the Nazi High Command firmly accepted *The Coming Race* as total, complete evidence of the existence of a New Race beneath the earth.

They also accepted Bulwer Lytton's version of the genesis of the cavern people. Nazi records seized after the fall of the Third Reich indicate that Hitler and his henchmen launched several unsuccessful expedition to the hollow earth. Frustrated German geographers and scientists were ordered to find tunnel entrances that led to Vril-ya. German, Swiss, and Italian mines were charted for possible shafts leading down to the interior land of cavern cities. Hitler even ordered an intellectually-inclined Army Colonel to check out Bulwer Lytton's life, hoping to find where – and when – the author had visited the caverns of the Vril-ya.

Admittedly, there was a considerable amount of pseudoscience under Hitler's regime in Germany. It is astonishing that the brutal men who sent an invasion of jack-booted armies across Europe believed in Lytton's genesis of the Vril-ya.

Lytton's explanation of how the Vril-ya arrived in the interior is as follows:

> It was not for some time, and until, by repeated trances, if they are so to be called, my mind became bet-

ter prepared to interchange ideas with my entertainers, and more fully to comprehend differences of manners and customs, at first too strange to my experience to be seized by my reason, that I was enabled to gather the following details respecting the origin and history of this subterranean population, as portion of one great family race called the Ana.

According to the earliest traditions, the remote progenitors of the race had once tenanted a world above the surface of that in which their descendants dwelt. Myths of that world were still preserved in their archives, and in those myths were legends of a vaulted dome in which the lamps were lighted by no human hand. But such legends were considered by most commentators as allegorical fables. According to these traditions the earth itself, at the date to which the traditions refer, was not indeed in its infancy, but in the throes and travail of transition from one form of development to another, and subject to many violent revolutions of nature. By one of such revolutions, that portion of the upper world inhabited by the ancestors of this race had been subjected to inundations, not rapid, but gradual and uncontrollable, in which all, save a scanty remnant, were submerged and perished.

Whether this be a record of our historical and sacred Deluge, or of some earlier one contended for by geologists, I do not pretend to conjecture; though, according to the chronology of this people as compared with that of Newton, it must have been many thousands of years before the time of Noah. On the other hand, the account of these writers does not harmonise with the opinions most in vogue, among geological authorities, inasmuch as it places the existence of a human race upon the earth at dates long anterior to that assigned to the terrestrial formation adapted to the introduction of mammalia.

A band of the ill-fated race, thus invaded by the Flood, had, during the march of the waters, taken refuge in caverns amidst the loftier rocks, and, wandering through these hollows, they lost sight of the upper world forever. Indeed, the whole face of the earth had been changed by this great revolution; land had been turned into sea – sea into land.

In the bowels of the inner earth even now, I was informed as a positive fact, might be discovered the remains of human habitation – habitation not in huts and caverns, but in vast cities whose ruins attest the civilisation of races which flourished before the age of Noah, and are not to be classified with those to which philosophy ascribes the use of flint and the ignorance of iron.

The fugitives had carried with them the knowledge of the arts they had practised above ground – arts of culture and civilisation. Their earliest want must have been that of supplying below the earth the light they had lost above it; and at no time, even in the traditional period, do the races, of which the one I now sojourned with formed a tribe, seem to have been unacquainted with the art of extracting light from gases, or manganese, or petroleum.

They had been accustomed in their former state to contend with the rude forces of nature; and indeed the lengthened battle they had fought with their conqueror Ocean, which had taken centuries in its spread, had quickened their skill in curbing waters into dikes and channels. To this skill they owed their preservation in their new abode.

'For many generations,' said my host, with a sort of contempt and horror, 'these primitive forefathers are said to have degraded their ranks and shortened their lives by eating the flesh of animals, many varieties of which had, like themselves, escaped the Deluge, and sought shelter in the hollows of the earth; other animals, supposed to be unknown to the upper world, those hollows themselves produced.'

When what we should term the historical age emerged

from the twilight of tradition, the Ana were already established in different communities, and had attained to a degree of civilisation very analogous to that which the more advanced nations above the earth now enjoy.

They were familiar with most of our mechanical inventions, including the application of steam as well as gas. The communities were in fierce competition with each other. They had their rich and their poor; they had orators and conquerors; they made war either for a domain or an idea. Though the varous states acknowledged various forms of government, free institutions were beginning to preponderate; popular assemblies increased in power; republics soon became general; the democracy to which the most enlightened European politicians look forward as the extreme goal of political advancement, and which still prevailed among other subterranean races, whom they despised as barbarians, the loftier family of Ana, to which belonged the tribe I was visiting, looked back to as one of the crude and ignorant experiments which belong to the infancy of political science.

It was the age of envy and hate, of fierce passions, of constant social changes more or less violent, of strife between classes, of war between state and state. This phase of society lasted, however, for some ages, and was finally brought to a close, at least among the nobler and more intellectual populations, by the gradual discovery of the latent powers stored in the all-permeating fluid which they denominate Vril.

According to the account I received from Zee, who, as an erudite professor in the College of Sages, had studied such matters more diligently than any other member of my host's family, this fluid is capable of being raised and disciplined into the mightiest agency over all forms of matter, animate or inanimate. It can destroy like the flash of lightning; yet, differently applied, it can replenish or invigorate life, heal, and preserve, and on it they chiefly rely for the cure of disease, or rather for enabling the physical organisation to reestablish the due equilibrium of its natural powers, and thereby to cure itself.

By this agency they rend way through the most solid substances, and open valleys for culture through the rocks of their subterranean wilderness. From it they extract the light which supplies their lamps, finding it steadier, softer, and healthier than the other inflammable materials they had formerly used.

But the effects of the alleged discovery of the means to direct the more terrible force of vril were chiefly remarkable in their influence upon social polity. As these effects became familiarly known and skillfully administered, war between the Vril-discoverers ceased, for they brought the art of destruction to such perfection as to annul all superiority in numbers, discipline, or military skill. The fire lodged in the hollow of a rod directed by the hand of a child could shatter the strongest fortress, or cleave its burning way from the van to the rear of an embattled host. If army met army, and both had command of this agency, it could be but to the annihilation of each.

The age of war was therefore gone, but with the cessation of war other effects bearing upon the social state soon became apparent. Man was so completely at the mercy of man, each whom he encountered being able, if so willing, to slay him on the instant, that all notions of government by force gradually vanished from political systems and forms of law. It is only by force that vast communities, dispersed through great distances of space, can be kept together; but now there was no longer either the necessity of self-preservation or the pride of aggrandisement to make one state desire to preponderate in population over another.

The Vril-discoverers thus, in the course of a few generations, peacefully split into communities of moderate size. The tribe amongst which I had fallen was limited to 12,000 families. Each tribe occupied a territory sufficient for all its wants, and at stated periods the surplus population departed to seek a realm of its own. There appeared no necessity for any arbitrary selection of these emigrants; there was always a sufficient number who volunteered to depart.

These subdivided states, petty if we regard either territory or population – all appertained to one vast general family. They spoke the same language, though the dialects might slightly differ. They intermarried, they maintained the same general laws and customs; and so important a bond between these several communities was the knowledge of vril and the practice of its agencies, that the word A-Vril was synonymous with civilisation; and Vril-ya, signifying 'The Civilised Nations,' was the common name by which the communities employing the uses of vril distinguished themselves from such of the Ana as were yet in a state of barbarism.

The government of the tribe of Vril-ya I am treating of was apparently very complicated, really very simple. It was based upon a principle recognised in theory, though little carried out in practice, above ground – viz., that the object of all systems of philosophical thought tends to the attainment of unity, or the ascent through all intervening labyrinths to the simplicity of a single first cause or principle. Thus in politics, even republican writers have agreed that a benevolent autocracy would insure the best administration, if there were any guarantees for its continuance, or against its gradual abuse of the powers accorded to it.

This singular community elected therefore a single supreme magistrate called Tur; he held his office nominally for life, but he could seldom be induced to retain it after the first approach of old age. There was indeed in this society nothing to induce any of its members to covet the cares of office. No honours, no insignia of higher rank, were assigned to it. The supreme magistrate was not distinguished from the rest by superior habitation or revenue. On the other hand, the duties awarded to him were marvellously light and easy, requiring no preponderant degree of energy or intelligence. There being no apprehensions of war, there were no armies to maintain; being no government by force, there was no police to appoint and direct.

What we call crime was utterly unknown to the Vril-ya; and there were no courts of criminal justice. The rare instances of civil disputes were referred for arbitration to friends chosen by either party, or decided by the Council of Sages, which will be described later. There were no professional lawyers; and indeed their laws were but amicable conventions, for there was no power to enforce laws against an offender who carried in his staff the power to destroy his judges.

There were customs and regulations in compliance with which, for several ages, the people had tacitly habituated themselves; or if in any instance an individual felt such compliance hard, he quitted the community and went elsewhere.

There was, in fact, quietly established amid this state, much the same compact that is found in our private families, in which we virtually say to any independent grown-up member of the family whom we receive and entertain, 'stay or go, according as our habits and regulations suit or displease you.'

But though there were no laws such as we call laws, no race above ground is so law-observing. Obedience to the rule adopted by the community has become as much an instinct as if it were implanted by nature. Even in every household the head of it makes a regulation for its guidance, which is never resisted nor even cavilled at by those who belong to the family.

They have a proverb, the pithiness of which is much lost in this paraphrase, 'No happiness without order, no order without authority, no authority without unity.' The mildness of all government among them, civil or domestic, may be signalised by their idiomatic expressions for such terms as illegal or forbidden – viz, 'It is requested not to do so-and-so.' Poverty among the Ana is as unknown as crime; not that property is held in common, or that all are equals in the extent of their possessions or the size and luxury of their habitations; but there being no difference of rank or position between the grades of wealth or the choice of occupations, each pursues his own inclinations without creating envy or vying; some like a modest, some a more splendid kind of life; each makes himself happy in his own way.

Owing to this absence of competition, and the limit placed on the population, it is difficult for a family to fall into distress; there are no hazardous speculations, no emulators striving for superior wealth and rank. No doubt, in each settlement all originally had the same proportions of land dealt out to them; but some, more adventurous than others, had extended their possessions further into the bordering wilds, or had improved into richer fertility the produce of their fields, or entered into commerce or trade.

Thus, necessarily, some had grown richer than others, but none had become absolutely poor, or wanting anything which their tastes desired. If they did so, it was always in their power to migrate, or at the worst to apply, without shame and with certainty of aid, to the rich; for all the members of the community considered themselves as brothers of one affectionate and united family.

The chief care of the supreme magistrate was to communicate with certain active departments charged with the administraion of special details. The most important and essential of such details was that connected with the due provision of light. Of this department my host, Aph-Lin, was the chief. Another department, which might be called the foreign, communicated with the neighbouring kindred states, principally for the purpose of ascertaining all new inventions; and to a third department, all such inventions and improvements in machinery were committed for trial.

Connected with this department was the College of Sages – a college especially favoured by such of the Ana as were widowed and childless, and by the young unmarried females amongst whom Zee was the most active, and, if what we call renown or distinction was a thing acknowledged by this people, among the most renowned or distinguished. It is by the female Professors of this College that those studies which are deemed of least use in practical life – as purely speculative philosophy, the history of remote periods, and such sciences as entomology, conchology, etc. – are the more diligently cultivated.

Zee, whose mind, active as Aristotle's, equally embraced the largest domains and the minutest details of thought, had written two volumes on the parasite insect that dwells amid the hairs of a tiger's paw, which work was considered the best authority on that interesting subject.

(The animal here referred to has many points of difference from the tiger of the upper world. It is larger, and with a broader paw, and still more receeding frontal. It haunts the sides of lakes and pools, and feeds principally on fishes, though it does not object to any terrestrial animal of inferior strength that comes in its way. It is becoming very scarce even in the wild districts, where it is devoured by gigantic reptiles. I apprehend that it clearly belongs to the tiger species, since the parasite animalcule found in its paw, like that found in the Asiatic tiger's, is a miniature image of itself.)

But the researches of the sages are not confined to such subtle or elegant studies. They comprise various others more important, and especially the properties of vril, to the perception of which their finer nervous organisation renders the female Professors eminently keen. It is out of this college that the Tur, or chief magistrate, selects Councillors, limited to three, in the rare instances in which novelty of event or circumstance perplexes his own judgment.

There are a few other departments of minor consequence, but all are carried on so noiselessly and quietly that the evidence of a government seems to vanish altogether, and social order to be as regular and unobtrusive as if it were a law of nature. Machinery is employed to an inconceivable extent in all the operations of labour within and without doors, and it is the unceasing object of the department charged with its adminstration to extend its efficiency.

There is no class of laborers or servants, but all who are required to assist or control the machinery are found in the children, from the time they leave the care of their mothers to the marriageable age, which they place at sixteen for the Gy-ei (the females), twenty for the Ana (the males). These children are formed into bands and sections under their own chiefs, each following the pursuits in which he is most pleased, or for which he feels himself most fitted. Some take to handicrafts, some to agriculture, some to household work, and some to the only services of danger to which the population is exposed. The sole perils that threaten this tribe are, first, from those occasional convulsions within the earth, to foresee and guard against with their utmost ingenuity – irruptions of fire and water, the storms of subterranean winds and escaping gases.

At the borders of the domain, and at all places where such peril might be apprehended, vigilant inspectors are stationed with telegraphic communications to the hall in which chosen sages take it by turns to hold perpetual sittings. These inspectors are always selected from the elder boys approaching the age of puberty, and on the principle that at that age observation is more acute and the physical forces more alert than at any other. The second service of danger, less grave, is in the destruction of all creatures hostile to the life, or the culture, or even the comfort, of the Ana. Of these the most formidable are the vast reptiles, of some of which antediluvian relics are preserved in our museums, and certain gigantic winged creatures, half bird, half reptile.

These, together with lesser wild animals, corresponding to our tigers or venomous serpents, it is left to the younger children to hunt and destroy; because, according to the Ana, here ruthlessness is wanted, and the younger a child the more ruthlessly he will destroy. There is another class of animals in the destruction of which discrimination is to be used, and against which children of intermediate age are appointed – animals that do not threaten the life of man, but ravage the produce of his labour, varieties of the elk and deer species, and a smaller creature much akin to our rabbit, though infinitely more destructive to crops, and much more cunning in its mode of depredation.

It is the first object of these appointed infants, to tame the more intelligent of such animals into respect for enclosures signalised by conspicuous landmarks, as dogs are taught to respect a larder, or even to guard the master's property. It is only where such creatures are found untamable to the extent that they are destroyed. Life is never taken away for food or for sport, and never spared where untamably inimical to the Ana. Concomitantly with these bodily services and tasks, the mental education of the children goes on till boyhood ceases.

It is the general custom, then, to pass through a course of instruction at the College of Sages, in which, besides more general studies, the pupil receives special lessons in such vocation or direction of intellect as he himself selects. Some, however, prefer to pass this period of probation in travel, or to emigrate, or to settle down at once into rural or commercial pursuits. No force is put upon individual inclination.

ADOLF HITLER: MESSIAH OF HOLLOW EARTH LORE

Adolf Hitler and his aides boasted that their Third Reich would endure for a thousand years. Their plans called for a splendid civilization ruled by a master race of pure-blooded Aryans, surpassing the splendor of Rome, and all other nations. How do you obtain the plans for such a bold project? Where do you obtain the blueprints for a society ruled by self-styled God-men? How do you blueprint the social structure of an enduring civilization? Hitler and his henchmen turned to Bulwer Lytton's *The Coming Race*, Buddhist orders, and the *Vril-ya* for their initial plans.

Lytton's *Vril-ya* considered democracy, free institutions, and a Republic type of government as 'one of the crude and ignorant experiments which belong to the infancy of political science.' Might was translated to right by Hitler; he argued that a dictatorship was the only pure form of intelligent rule for a modern nation. As the small nations of Europe fell before his armies of black-booted invaders, Hitler ruled by force. In *The Coming Race*, Lytton's 'Tur,' the Supreme Magistrate, was a dictatorial figure. The *Vril-ya* bowed to their 'Tur . . . or, head of the household,' just as the citizens of Germany delivered themselves and their fate to the Third Reich.

'No happiness without order, no order without authority, no authority without unity' was translated into a Hitlerian blueprint for Germany. The Germans have always been an island between the cultures of the East and West. Western nations have stressed reason, liberty for the individual, democracy, and strict adherence to constitutional equality. In the East, people accepted strongmen as their leaders. Emperors ruled in China, War-lords in the Mongolian wastelands, and the power of life-or-death was given to a Russian Czar, or a Communist bureaucrat. Whatever they called their dictators, the Eastern nations worshipped their leaders, accepted dictators, and bowed to the might of the state. Hitler, who was a mystic, tossed an umbrella of Eastern philosophy over his Third Reich. He convinced the German people that their troubles would end when he brought order, authority, and unity to their nation. They accepted this evil messiah and his evil followers.

Lytton's inner earth civilization placed little emphasis on riches and material gains. The Third Reich, in turn, gave their highest honors to Nazi party members and sacrificial heroes. Medals, awards, and honors were bestowed on Hitler's favorites. 'There was political chaos in Germany after World War One,' said Gunther Rosenberg, of the European Occult Research Society. 'Hitler preyed on the fears and frustrations of the people. A man might be unable to compete in society, but he could serve the Nazi party as a political hack and obtain recognition. He could strut in parades, his chest decorated with a dozen elaborate medals.'

The Third Reich recognized the power of womanhood and requested German girls to honor Nazi heroes, father a 'New Race of blood-pure Aryans,' and sacrifice their lives to Hitler's conquests. At the same time, Hitler's 'Youth Corps' were formed into groups dedicated to the fatherland, brainwashed by Nazi propaganda, based on false racial superiority. The *Vril-ya* used young children for observation at frontier outposts; Hitler had German boys and girls act as the eyes and ears of his party. Misguided children turned their parents and relatives over to Nazi authorities as 'enemies of the state.' A critic of Hitler's regime guarded his tongue – even at home.

The *Vril-ya* believed in the total ruthlessness of children and the Nazis translated this into Hitler's corps of adolescent 'werewolves,' sinister young boys in black uniforms and a death's head insignia on their sleeves. And, of course, behind the might of the German war machine were the slave laborers to perform menial tasks – or be the victims of some bizarre medical experiment by a Nazi doctor. They would *serve* until the Vril power was discovered.

Before you doubt that Hitler's Third Reich was based on black occult lore, let's look at some remarkable sidelights to European history. Europeans have frequently been fascinated by many elements of the occult, forming secret societies, developing new theories, and accepting some self-styled holy man as a messiah.

'To understand the links between *The Coming Race*, the Hollow Earth and Hitler,' said Gunther Rosenberg, 'we must go back to England around 1885 when a group of important people formed a society of initiates known as the *Golden Dawn*. The group was formed for the practice of ceremonial magic and W. B. Yeats, the Nobel prize winner, presided as the chief magician. Yeats wore a long black robe, a mask, and performed a ritual with a golden dagger.'

The *Golden Dawn* was limited to 144 members, primarily writers, artists, and English leaders. One of the most prominent members was Bulwer Lytton, who wrote *The Coming Race*, Bram Stoker, who wrote *Dracula*, Sax Rohmer, and Sir Gerald Kelly, who was then president of the Royal Academy, were members. So were Wynn Westcoot, a reknowned occultist, and Arthur Machen, the author of several occult books. The *Golden Dawn* society was established by Samuel Mathers, who swore he had been contacted by a group of 'Superior Beings' or 'Supermen.' He said these contacts had been made in the presence of his wife; Mrs. Mathers was a sister of Henri Bergson, the French philosopher.

Who were these supermen? Mathers described them in a letter to his 'Members of the Second Order':

> As to the Secret Chiefs with whom I am in touch and from whom I have received the wisdom of the Second Order which I communicated to you, I can tell you noththing. I do not even know their earthly names, and I have

very seldom seen them in their physical bodies . . . They used to meet me physically at a time and place established in advance. As for me, I believe they are human beings living on this earth, but endowed with terrible, supernatural powers . . . My meetings with them have shown me how difficult it is for a mortal man, however 'advanced', to be in their presence . . . I don't mean that during my rare encounters with them that I experienced the same feeling of intense physical depression that is accompanied by the loss of magnetism . . .

. . . On the contrary, I felt I was before a force so great that I can only compare it with a shock one would receive by being close to a flash of lightning during a great thunderstorm and, at the same time, experiencing great difficulty in breathing . . . The nervous symptoms I spoke of were accompanied by the cold sweats, bleeding from the mouth, nose, and sometimes the ears.

'It was only natural that the *Golden Dawn* initiates considered these supermen as possible emissaries from the hollow earth,' declared Gunther Rosenberg. 'Bulwer Lytton's book had been discussed on many occasions by *Golden Dawn* members; many felt he had been in contact with these same beings and *The Coming Race* was based on an actual experience.'

Throughout its existence, the *Golden Dawn* society maintained close contact with occult groups in other countries, including Germany. One of the earliest members of the German *Golden Dawn* was Karl Haushofer, a professor at the University of Munich.

Born in 1869, Karl Haushofer was one of those enigmatic figures in history who are frequently dismissed by traditional historians. However, this unusual man may have been the major influence on Hitler. 'In fact, Haushofer visited Hitler when he was in prison after the abortive beer hall *putsch* in Munich in 1923. Rudolph Hess, Hitler's assistant, had been an aide to Haushofer when he was a professor,' explained Gunther Rosenberg. 'By 1914, Haushofer was a general in the Germany army. He advised Hitler to write his book, *Mein Kampf*.'

General Karl Haushofer had visited India, China, and Tibet, on several trips to the Far East. He learned the languages and adopted Buddhist beliefs. 'He was initiated into a powerful secret Buddhist society during a trip to Japan,' said Gunther Rosenberg. 'He was given a mission with death-by-suicide as the consequence for failure.' While he toured Asia, Haushofer became intrigued by the Oriental legend of Agharta and the reported subterranean cities beneath the mountains.

'General Haushofer believer that the German people were originally from Central Asia,' said Gunther Rosenberg. 'As early as 1905, he declared that Agharta and Shamballah were real, that they existed under the Himalayan mountains, and there was a 'white' and 'black' order, good and evil.'

Following World War I and Germany's defeat, Haushofer resumed his studies of occult lore, religion, and geography. 'He developed some theories of political geography known as geo-politics,' said Gunther Rosenberg. 'He believed that 'control areas' of the world existed. Whatever nation possessed them would control the world.

Geo-politics was originated by Sir Halford J. MacKinder, who expressed his theories in 'who rules the Heartland commands the World Island; who rules the World Island commands the world.' MacKinder was never too precise on the exact location of the 'heartland.' Karl Haushofer, under the psychic spell of eastern mysticism, knew exactly where the 'heartland' rested. 'It is in Mongolia,' he wrote in his magazine, *The Geo-Political Review*.' He who controls Mongolia will rule the world.'

General Haushofer's mystical talents brought him considerable fame in Germany. He was capable of predicting events in advance of their occurrence. 'He was known as a general with second sight,' said Gunther Rosenberg. 'On the battlefield, he predicted accurately the time when an enemy attack would occur. He could walk over the trenches and point out the spots where enemy shells would land. He seemed aware of political changes many months, even years, before they became reality. Based on our research, we concluded that Haushofer was certainly psychically gifted.'

The German people felt that Adolf Hitler was also gifted with the power to see into the future. His remarkable statement of his intentions in *Mein Kampf* occurred on schedule, up to the demise of the Third Reich. He predicted in advance when Nazi troops would conquer Paris, the German occupation of the Rhineland, and the date of President Roosevelt's death.

'Hitler was born in Braumau-am-Inn, a frontier town on the Austrian border,' reported Rosenberg. 'Besides being noted as the birthplace of the German *fuhrer*, the town had an occult reputation as an area where psychics, mediums, and seers were born. Willi and Rudi Scheneider were both born there, two of the most remarkable mediums in modern history.'

Was Hitler a medium or was Haushofer the man behind the scenes who fed predictions to the little dictator? 'We've never been able to determine if Haushofer was the black magician who controlled Hitler,' said Rosenberg. 'After his flight to England, Rudolph Hess is supposed to have told British Intelligence that Haushofer was the power, the brains, possibly the magician, behind Hitler and his demonic legions.'

Even the symbol of the Nazi legions is said to have been selected by Karl Haushofer. 'Haushofer knew that the swastika was a powerful, magical sign in both Europe and Asia,' said Dr. Rosenberg. 'He felt the swastika linked Germany to their mystical ties with ancient Asia.'

When Hitler, who was possibly directed by Haushofer, started his battle to power in Germany, he frequently obtained readings from mediums in Berlin. 'There was a Tibetan monk in Berlin known as the 'Magician with the Blue Robe.' Hitler consulted him regularly,' Gunther Rosenberg revealed. 'The Tibetan also made several public predictions that were printed by Nazi newspapers. These included the number of Hitler's deputies who would be elected to the Reichstag.' The Nazi propaganda papers reported that the monk 'knew the secret of the entrances to Agharta.'

By 1925, when Ossendowski's *Men, Beasts, and Gods* brought even more attention to the hollow earth theory, a new group of Tibetan monks came out of Asia and took up residence in Berlin. 'They were members of the black orders, who swore allegiance to the powers of darkness,' Rosenberg stated. 'From the day they moved to Berlin, the Nazis made certain funds available to finance expeditions to Tibet and Mongolia.'

Rosenberg reported that his organization learned that Tibetan mysticism was the source of inspiration for the Nazi regime and Third Reich. 'When Berlin fell to the Allied armies, all of Germany was in turmoil,' said Rosenberg. 'Archives were being destroyed by the Nazis. The French, Americans, British, and Russians vied with each other to obtain Nazi documents. The documents were carried back to the different countries. Since then, we have checked the sources that have been available. The entire Nazi movement was based on this Tibetan esotericism.'

When Germany fell, Berlin was a smouldering city assaulted by the modern weapons of warfare. Allied tanks rumbled through the streets. Russian Yak planes roared through the skies, firing tracer bullets and bombing anything that moved on the ground. The center of the Third Reich was in flames. The *fuhrer* was dead from a suicide shot from a Walther pistol. 'And in the rubble of Berlin were hundreds of thousands of Nazi warriors,' related Gunther Rosenberg. 'Among them were several hundred volunteers in the black uniform of the S. S. death's head division. They were Orientals, without badges, papers, or any kind of identification. They were the last of the black monks who had helped Hitler's dark, menacing movement.'

General Karl Haushofer outlived his fellow initiates in

Nazi mysticism, solemnly watching the destruction of the Nazi dream. 'He had mixed ceremonial magic, occult lore, and mysticism into a racial war against humanity,' related Gunther Rosenberg. 'We may never know the full breadth of his influence.'

On March 14, 1946, Haushofer killed his wife. Calm and serene, he walked quietly to a ceremonial prayer rug, knelt before a Buddhistic altar from the black order, and inserted a knife in his abdomen – Japanese *Hari kari*.

'His son, Albrecht, knew Haushofer much better than anyone realized,' said Gunther Rosenberg. 'Albrecht knew his father had been the original magician behind the Nazi monster. Albrecht was in on the bomb plot to kill Hitler on July 20, 1944. He was executed following his arrest.'

A blood-stained poem was taken from Albrecht Haushofer's pocket. It read:

For my father destiny has spoken;
Once again, the demons had to be defeated
and entombed in his cell . . .
My father deliberately broke thc seal—
He dismissed and did not feel the Demon's breath,
And set him free to roam the world . . .

Pseudo-science and some of the most preposterous proposals in history received serious consideration in Hitler's Germany. Mystical belief in the old Gods of Teutonic mythology had always intrigued the Germanic nation. 'The Germans have one foot mired in the legend of Atlantis, the other foot in Western culture, and their face is turned eastward in prayer to the mystic lore of the Orient,' said Albert McDonald, president of the Hollow Earth Society.

'The Third Reich was a system where the cranks, eccentrics, and crack-pots were in charge of an entire country,' Gunther Rosenberg reported. Every city has a few of these people who build their lives around unproven, often bizarre beliefs. In your country, the cultists of California are noted for their weird beliefs. England has the prophets and crack-pots speaking in Hyde Park. In your American city of Chicago, which I visited a few years ago, there was a delightful area known as Bug-House Square. The place was swarming with visionaries, prophets, and crack-pots when I was there. The gadflies, off-beat theorists, and far-out philosophers have a place in our world. We should protect their right to expound their eccentric views. But, Germany was under the direction of these people. Hitler and his fanatic aides believed they were correct in their weird theories of science.'

How fervent was the Nazi belief in a hollow earth?

Let's go back to 1942 when the German High Command suffered their first military defeats. The Russians had launched a massive attack and freed Leningrad from a German seige. Tired, cold, and defeated, twenty crack German divisions surrendered to the Russians at Stalingrad. America had entered the war against the Nazis and a resistance movement mushroomed in the occupied countries. Soldiers in France, Poland, Denmark, Yugoslavia, and other countries were confronted with sabotage, sniper attacks, and deadly night bombings. Time was desperately needed for work on the V-2 rocket program, atomic energy, and new weaponry.

Yet, in January, 1942, *Reichsfuhrer* Heinrich Himmler and four black-shirted bodyguards strode into a meeting with Adolf Hitler and Nazi propagandist, Josef Goebbels. Himmler, who looked like a quiet, mild-mannered professor, was the most deadly mass murderer of all time. An ex-chicken farmer, Himmler was supreme commander of the deadly S.S., the *Schultz-Staffen.*

Goebbels and Himmler had been summoned to Hitler's headquarters by an urgent message. Hitler stressed the importance of the meeting. He had to bring victory to his master race.

Himmler was fitful and nervous. He was charged with the execution of millions of Jews, and sometimes, he complained about his role as official killer. 'No one knows how difficult it can be to obtain an efficient operation,' he complained.

Goebbels, a dwarf of a man with large eyes and a strangely shaped head, jumped up and saluted Hitler when the *fuhrer* entered the room. Hitler acknowledged the greetings from his officers. He slumped down in a chair at the end of the polished conference table. A portrait of Bismark glared down on the group from a far wall.

'I have been given some new scientific information,' Hitler said. 'We have just learned that the earth is concave, not convex. We are not living on the outside of this planet, but on the inside. Man is like a nest of insects crawling on the inside of a crystal bowl.'

'Has this been proved scientifically?' asked Goebbels.

'It has been developed by several scientists of the National-Socialist party,' replied Hitler. 'Now, we must make tests to demonstrate the truth of the plan.'

'Who can do this?' asked Himmler. 'Whatever we need will be put to the task.'

Within the hour a radio message from Hitler's staff went out to a selected number of German radar technicians and scientists:

HOLD IN ABEYANCE ALL RESEARCH UNTIL FURTHER ORDERS. REPORT TO BERLIN FOR IMMEDIATE ASSIGNMENT. MAINTAIN CONTACT AND BE PREPARED TO REMAIN IN BERLIN FOR TWO WEEKS.

Some of the greatest experts on radio, infra-red rays, and photography were gathered in Berlin. They were outfitted and equipped for an expedition to Rugen Island in the Baltic Sea. Radar instruments were pulled out of Germany's defense units; Nazi industry was cannibalized for scientific instruments. The German Admiralty directed the expedition, which was considered of vital importance to a German war victory.

In April, 1942, scientists and technicians set up their equipment on Rugen. Radar units were aimed at the sky at a sharp angle. Security agents from the S.S. roamed around the scientists to maintain secrecy. On the shore, stone-faced German army sentries guarded the expedition from possible Commando raids from the Allies.

The mystified scientists left the radar in a single position for a week.

'The theory was that radar rays travelled in a straight line so it would be possible to obtain a reading on an area beyound the horizon,' explained Dr. Gunther Rosenberg. 'In other words, by bouncing radar rays off the top of Hitler's "bowl," they could obtain a reflected reading of the British fleet and its positions. It was one of the most fantastic theories in history.'

The Nazi expedition returned to Berlin without verifying Hitler's belief in a hollow earth. In a monograph on the subject published by the European Occult Research Society, a researcher remarked: 'This unsuccessful experiment failed to dim the Nazi belief in a hollow earth. High leaders in the German General Staff, the Admiralty, and the Air Force denied that the earth is round and discussed their beliefs in a hollow planet. They believed the Rugen test would be useful for locating the British fleet. The concave curvature of our planet, as Hitler saw it, would lead to observations over long distances through infra-red rays, which curve less than rays that are visible.'

The crack-pot scientists who brought the idea to Hitler claimed that our world is a globe inside an enormous rock. There is no universe or outer space; the rock stretches onward forever. The sky is the center of our world, a mass of blue-gray gasses. The stars are not distant planets, but pinpoints of light streaming through the gasses above us. True, there is a sun and moon, as the astronomers claimed, but both planetary bodies were much smaller than science realized. The entire universe is nothing but an infinite mass of rock.

'Following the debacles at Rugen, Hitler became enraged at his so-called scientific advisers,' reported Gunther Rosenberg. 'Several of these believers in a rock universe were shipped off to concentration camps. There, Himmler's death's head division of S.S. murdered them and scattered their remains to the wind. Yet, despite this setback Hitler and the Nazis continued to believe in a hollow earth.'

Hitler, Himmler, Goebbels, and Haushofer were intrigued by the Buddhistic belief in subterranean tunnels beneath the earth. 'As early as 1936, the Nazis were sending teams of elite corpsmen into caves and mines in Europe,' Rosenberg said. 'They were checking on a possible entrance into the land of the *Vril-ya*. Entire crews of spelunkers prowled caves hunting for the new, advanced man.'

Rosenberg stated that as the Allied armies advanced toward Berlin, elite S.S. men made preparations for an escape from the ruined nations. 'Hitler was interested in an act of Godly creation,' said Dr. Rosenberg. 'He wanted to create a vast Third Reich that would rule for a thousand years – or until the Supreme beings came to meet with man. He also became obsessed with mutant man, a mixture of human being and gods. A God-man. When vowed to bring down the world with him, rather than surrender, he allowed Germany to be pulverized by the Allied armies.'

On March 14, 1939, Hitler's legions marched into Czechoslovakia and seized the capital city, Prague. The country was placed under German control. As the swastika flag was draped over the buildings in Prague, a special group of S.S. men were ordered into the defeated country. Directed by an S.S. *Obergruppenfuhrer* (Lieutenant General), the group was personally supervised by Heinrich Himmler, S.S. director. A crackpot visionary and believer in the hollow earth, Himmler personally selected his group for the Czech operation.

Their goal? 'Himmler's S.S. organization had collected folk tales from throughout Europe of weird caves, tunnels, and haunted mines,' said Gunther Rosenberg. 'One of their most promising areas was several regions in Czechoslovakia with ancient legends about prehistoric civilizations and superior beings who lived beneath the earth.'

Some of the most famous military men in Prussian-Junker

history encouraged Himmler in his quest for a subterranean paradise. 'The Third Reich was totally out of touch with reality,' Rosenberg stated. 'Some even imagined that Himmler might reach an interior land, negotiate a treaty with the inhabitants, and return with the famed *Vril* power source.'

Although the Czech venture failed, the cave sought by Himmler's men may have been accidentally discovered by Dr. Antonin T. Horak, a Captain in the Slovak Uprising during World War II. Dr. Horak, who is now a linguist, has attempted for several years to get speleologists and cave experts to investigate what he believes is one of the underworld's strangest mysteries. His experience was originally published in the March, 1965, issue of the *NSS News*, a publication of the National Speleological Society. The cave is said to be located near the settlements of Plavince and Lubocna, in an area about 49.2 degrees north, 20.7 degrees east.

After a fire fight, Horak and the remnants of a battalion of resistance fighters were moving back along a snow-covered slope. They were given assistance and led to a cave shelter by a peasant family. Horak, a companion named Jurek, and a wounded man, Martin, were led to a large underground grotto.

'Don't go any further into the cave,' cautioned the peasant. 'It is full of pits, poison gas pockets, and it is haunted.'

As he waited for his wounded companion, Martin, to pass a crisis, Dr. Horak explored the cave. After crawling through the passageways, he stood in awed wonder before a large, dark, silo-like cylinder. The bizarre structure, framed in white, appeared to be man-made. It had an estimated diameter of about 25 meters (approximately 1,000 inches or 80 feet). Stalagmites and stalactites had formed the white frame around the strange blue-black object.

Dr. Horak discovered a 'crack' in an edge of the structure, which he called 'a moon shaft.' He wrote:

'Lighting some torches I saw that I was in a spacious,

curved, black shaft formed by cliff-like walls which intersect and form a crescent-shaped, early vertical shaft . . . The floor in the incline (was) a solid lime 'pavement.'

The 'pavement' was reported too thick for a trench pick. Determined to obtain samples from the glass-like material in the shaft, Dr. Horak fired a bullet into the walls. The bullet slammed into the substance with a deafening, fiery impact. Dr. Horak described the results as '. . . sparks, roaring, no splinters, but a half-finger-long welt which gave a pungent smell.'

The wounded man, Martin, died in his sleep on October 27, 1944, Dr. Horak and Jurek prepared to move out after burying their friend under a grave beneath some pine trees.

After a restful night and breakfast, Dr. Horak deposited a record of his visit in the moon shaft. Afterwards, he wrote: '. . . I sat there by my fire speculating: What is this structure, with walls two meters thick and a shape that I cannot imagine of any purpose known now-adays? How far does it reach into the rocks? Is there more behind the 'moon shaft?' Which incident, or who, put it into this mountain? Is it a fossilized man-made object? Is there truth in legends, like Plato's, about long lost civilizations with magic technologies which our rationale cannot grasp or believe?

At the date of this writing, no one has ventured into the Tatra mountains of Czechoslovakia to examine the mysterious 'moon shaft.' Was this unusual shaft the prize sought by Himmler and his S.S. men? The questions asked by Dr. Horak remain unanswered.

When it became apparent that Germany would be defeated by the Allies, a select group of Nazis set up *Operation Odessa*. *Odessa* was the code-word for a network of escape routes out of the ruined nation. 'One persistent rumor in occultism is that Hitler, Martin Borrman, and many of the missing Nazis were spirited out of Germany,' reported Gunther Rosenberg. 'Some claim they are in South America and, as we know, Eichmann was found there. Other believers in the hollow earth theory claim a fleet of Nazi submarines took Hitler and his henchmen to a Nazi base set up under the ice cap at the South Pole.'

Since earliest times, there have been shadowy occult legends about other lands, hidden worlds, and superior beings from an advanced civilization. These God-men are supposed to reveal themselves someday and become benefactors for humanity and our society. These advanced beings are to direct us, guide us, toward greater enlightenment, higher spirituality, and advanced knowledge. Some believers claim these superior God-men are the benign masters who dwell in the inner earth. Others, particularly some UFO contactees, claim these superior people are cosmic creatures from some dim star in outer space. Others have discussed the fascinating possibility that these masterful creatures are transparent beings from another dimension.

Adolph Hitler, General Karl Haushofer, and many prominent Germans during the Nazi reign believed in 'black' Buddhist teachings, subterranean worlds, and the devastating power of demonic magic. They believed in Bulwer Lytton's book, *The Coming Race*, and *Vril* power. *Vril* was to be the ultimate weapon for their self-proclaimed master race.

Hitler's Third Reich disintegrated 25 years ago in the ashes of Berlin.

Unfortunately, the black occultists are still with us today.

EXODUS: DEMONS AND THE SHAVER MYSTERY

It was one of the most sensational, highly controversial, articles ever published in an American magazine. 'I Remember Lemuria' by Richard S. Shaver was published in the March, 1945 issue of *Amazing Stories* magazine, a Ziff-Davis publication. *Life* magazine tagged the Shaver Mystery as 'the most celebrated rumpus that rocked the science-fiction world' because author Richard Shaver claimed the story was fact, not fiction.

Life said: '. . . The Shaver Mystery concerned a race of mal-formed subhuman creatures called deros (from detrimental robots) who inhabited a vast system of underground cities all over the world. The original name of their habitat was Lemuria, and they had once been slaves of the Lemurian master race. But the master race had long since disappeared from the earth, leaving the ignorant and malicious deros in control of the great cities and wonderful machines it had built. Since then the deros occupied themselves mainly in persecuting the human race who lived on the crust of the earth above them. The deros were responsible for much of the evil in the world. Catastrophes, from shipwrecks to sprained ankles, were attributable to their influence. They often appeared on the surface of the earth and were sufficiently human in appearance to pass unnoticed in a crowd. But they performed most of their harassment by telepathy, rays, and other remote control devices from their subterranean homes. Their underground cities communicated with the surface through various caves which were extremely dangerous for human beings to enter.'

Albert McDonald and his Hollow Earth Society have published several monographs on the Shaver Mystery, as it is known to occult and science-fiction fans. The group has formulated a committee on the Shaver Mystery and, as a result, their files are a very complete source of material on the controversial tale. Selections from the monographs are published here as they appeared in the organization's literature:

Who are the dero?

Essentially, Shaver declared that the interior of the earth is laced with networks of gigantic caves. The total area of the caves is larger than the total area of land on the surface world. The inhabitants of this cavern world are known as the 'abandondero,' as they were abandoned when a mass exodus from the earth occurred approximately 12,000 years ago. The migration was necessary when the sun started to throw deadly radiation over the entire solar system, including our own planet.

These radio-active emissions from the sun lodged in the bodies of an 'immortal' race who lived on earth. Known as the Titans and the Atlans, these immortal people now live in the dark voids of space. Unable to stand a radioactive sun, the Atlans and Titans made an attempt to live in caverns deep inside the earth. There were cavities within the earth and, with machines and superior technology, they enlarged these spaces into vast caverns.

Why didn't the Titans and Atlans remain in the caverns?

Until the sun turned radio-active, they had lived for thousands of years. They were virtually immortal. The radio-activity poisoned their bones, brought on cellular destruction, and the aging process as we know it today.

The Atlans and Titans, advanced races, had higher knowledge, superior technology, and science. They decided to leave the earth and seek another planet as a home, preferably one without a sun. They settled on a dark planet that has no sun. With their race dying, they launched a massive effort to construct space ships. Time was limited. They could not build a fleet of ships to allow everyone to migrate, and as with any life-saving venture, only certain groups were allowed to migrate. The poor, the unfortunate, and those afflicted with radio-active diseases, were left in the caverns. This is why Shaver called them the 'abandondero.'

What happened to the abandoned people?

The Atlans and Titans fled because the caves were cut off from the sun. Healthful rays were necessary for zest, vitality, and a normal life. As the abandoned group wandered through the caverns, they evolved down into degenerate, idiotic midgets. Shaver says these bestial creatures are the 'dero.' Totally without goodness, they're evil demonic creatures.

Another, less populous group, are the 'teros.' They managed to ward off mental and physical degeneration through beneficial nutrients, chemicals, and ray machines. Despite their best technical and medical research, teros age quickly. They usually die by the time they reach 50 years of age. The tero are advanced thinkers, dedicated to good, and they are ruled by benign leaders.

If the tero are smarter, shouldn't they have out-witted the deadly dero?

The dero are the devil-men, a fast-growing race with delight in attacking, capturing, and torturing the tero. The tero have been scattered through the caves and caverns. They are often forced to hide from the devlish deros. The forces of evil rule much of the interior.

What makes the dero so dangerous?

When the Atlans and Titans flew to another planet, they left their marvelous machines. The dero are the heirs to some of the most advanced technology in the universe. This equipment was created by people who were virtually immortal; therefore, their machines were built to last for thousands of years. The deros use these machines and technical systems to attack surface *homo sapiens* and the tero.

What types of machines have been taken over by the dero?

Some of the most advanced equipment known to humanity. A partial list includes:

Flying machines: Several years before the first modern flying saucer was sighted by Kenneth Arnold on the west coast, Shaver described these vehicles as being abandoned by the elder race that migrated to the stars.

Ray machines: Telaug and vision ray machines can penetrate cavern walls and bring in views of the surface world. These vision units allow the devlish deros to see what people are doing at any time, at any place, in the surface world.

Projection Ray machines: These machines project weird, fantastic images and thoughts into the minds of innocent victims, victims often selected at random by the demented dero.

Tractor Ray Beams: A train is speeding across the surface of the world. In the dark recesses of his cavern, a dero focuses a tractor beam on a railroad switch. The track is opened; the train is derailed. The dero can instantly change highway traffic signals, sabotage industrial machinery, and ruin complex devices. Have you ever had a machine or object that refused to work, then performed marvelously when the repairman arrived? A dero may have been amusing himself.

Tractor Ray machines are used to throw open manhole covers, loosen a single step on a stairway, or sabotage a vital part on a speeding automobile.

Surgical Ray cannons: The dero enjoys projects of the most terrible nature. These devices were originally created to perform delicate surgical operations. Today, the dero focuses these instruments on a person to slice a delicate, essential nerve. Surgical rays are beamed on a single individual's head until the juices of his brain bubble and boil furiously.

Mental machines: These horrible devices create realistic illusions, nightmares, strange dreams, and compulsive behaviour in a victim. Many murderers have informed the police that I just got a sudden urge to kill.' Were they actually the target of a vicious dero mental machine?

Richard Shaver stated that the cavern people have been bequeathed death rays, gigantic machines for excavating caves, powerful weapons, and fleets of vehicles for driving through the caverns. He also said that some deros enjoy driving modern automobiles from the surface world. Is it possible that stolen cars are driven down into the tunnels? Fortunately, not all of the people in the caverns are dedicated to evil purposes.

What is a stim machine?

Shaver wrote of a pleasure stimulation machine which was used to revitalize sexual nature. Shaver claimed to have had a stim machine played on him during his visits to the caverns. '. . . a powerful augmentation of woman-life; to a hundred powers of natural love,' he wrote. 'There are no words to describe what this apparatus did for life'

Unfortunately, many of these stim machines have been captured by roving bands of deros. These complex mechanisms are used to create varied degrees of sexual intensity. The deros, who are totally degenerate, may spend their entire lives in a stim ray sex orgy. This debauchery can be heightened to such a degree, and prolonged for so many years, that the dero is deformed. They are transformed into even more frightening, more monstrous creatures. Perhaps a stim machine is addictive.

Does this mean they do not harm women on the surface world?

To the contrary, the dero kidnap nubile young women for their amusement in the caverns. Stim rays are played over their bodies. A frightened, prudish woman can be transformed into the depraved, willing participant in a dero orgy.

In the May, 1967, issue of the *Hollow Earth Bulletin* we printed portions of 'The Messerschmidt Manuscript.' A French woman, thought to have been killed, returned to her home in the suburbs of Paris with a frightening tale of being kidnapped and taken into the dero's lair. An edited version of her statement follows:

> There are those who will claim I am insane . . . They will testify that I am mentally ill and unable to remember those weeks in the caves. I wish I could erase those memories from my mind. But, the world must be warned. The monsters are down there. We must destroy them before they kidnap more women for their horrible purposes . . .
>
> I was a young woman of nineteen years of age in 1943, proud of my ability as a student, and eagerly looking forward to marrying a young man who planned to be a physician.
>
> One night we planned to meet at my fiance's office building, join another couple, and have dinner in a small cafe. We were not worried about the Nazis. I arrived a few minutes late at my fiance's office building and the old man who ran the elevator had left for the day. I decided to operate the lift for myself. I stepped inside to inspect the controls.
>
> There were no symbols to indicate whether the lift went up or down by moving the lever one way or another. Lighthearted and in love, I decided that if I ran the elevator into the basement, I could reverse the controls and go up to the other stories ...
>
> I made an error and the elevator stopped in a dark basement. I reversed the controls, but my hand slipped. I pushed on the 'down' control.

The elevator suddenly plunged down below the basement, falling through space as if the cable had broken. After a rapid drop, perhaps several hundred feet, the elevator stopped with a sudden lurch. I was so frightened as I fell onto the floor of the cage, sobbing and screaming.

Through my terror-stricken mind, I heard a loud, guttural noise on the other side of the elevator door. The elevator door was torn open with a vicious slam and I saw the most horrible beast in the world. The memory of that monster haunts my mind and, at night, I cannot sleep without sedatives or sleeping pills ...

His face was of a pale, whitish color. His short, twisted body was covered with thick, bristly hair. His eyes? piggish, insensitive to any emotion, and gleaming with evil lust. The creature was fat, almost bloated. There were terrible scars and running sores over most of his body. He had no neck, so his head was placed squarely atop his muscular shoulders.

The face was the most horrible portion of his terrible features. It was much too large for his body, totally devoid of hair. The skin was scarred and wrinkled. His nose was fashioned more like a snout. It was at least seven inches in length, a terrible thing hanging down over his lipless mouth. His nose ended about the middle of his chest. He was nude. His body looked as if he had never worn garments.

A filthy, animal-smell filled the elevator. Mercifully, I fainted into unconsciousness. I have never known what happened in the elevator. Did they use that for an entry into the outside world? I have thought about it and those elevator shafts may go down far into the earth at certain points.

When I recovered consciousness, I was lying on the polished stone floor of an immense cavern. There were several other women standing around in that dark corner and, as my eyes adjusted to the dimness, I saw that we were caged into one corner of a large cave. A metal gate, and bars, rose from the stone floor up to the ceiling. I suppressed an impulse to scream, thinking this terrible nightmare would end any instant.

Across the way, the devil-men were fighting over a carcass. It was some reptile-like animal which they hunted in the caverns. I learned later that if these reptiles became scarce, they crept up into Paris at night and captured human beings for their food. There were giant hooks on the walls, quite sharp, where they hung the bodies to drain. They collected the blood as a drink, fighting among themselves for the thick, red drippings.

There were about twenty women crowded into the cave. Most of them were totally mad; insane creatures who had lost their minds. They huddled in the cage, whimpering and crying. Others simply sat in mute catatonic shock. They were like living robots, with their emotions and human feelings destroyed by the horrible existence in the caverns.

I stood up, looking around for my clothing, which was gone. Trying to hide my nakedness, I walked to the front of the cage. Despite my fear, I shouted across the room to the group of monstrous beings. It was a moment of total unreality.

'The police will be looking for me,' I said. 'Release me, or I'll charge you with kidnapping.' My mind was like a taut string on a musical instrument, ready to snap at any moment.

The devil-man who had pulled me from the elevator grinned wickedly through his lipless mouth. He lurched up from where he had been gnawing on the carcass. I trembled with fear as he shuffled toward me. I moved back into the cage.

He spoke in a guttural growl, almost grunts.

This was a signal and the other women in the cage grabbed me. They pressed me against the bars of the cage. I passed once again into unconsciousness as the devil-man placed a dirty, hairy palm on my breast.

. . . I regained my senses once more that same night. I remember that seven or eight of the devil-men chased me round the cavern. They tossed me back and forth between each other, fondling my body, and – as they wished – carrying me off into a passageway for their private amusement.

After that first night, nothing they could do to me would kill the spirit of life within my body. I learned! Oh! How I learned. I put my mind elsewhere when they pulled me from the cages. I survived and retained my sanity by living in the past. When one of the lusting, evil monsters dragged me out of the cages for his pleasure, I went into a catatonic state. I relived the happy years of my childhood in my mind to retain my sanity. Or, I blanked out into unconsciousness.

Most of the women who had been captive for some time were in horrible physical condition. They had picked up the various infections and sores from the beasts. They had skin eruptions and bruises were all over their bodies. Many had lost weight, due to the mental strain, and the food. The men-beasts often forgot to feed us and, when they did, they threw a large chunk of meat into the cage. I never knew if the meat was human, or animal, and I became so hungry that I didn't care.

About once a week, perhaps more often because time measurement was impossible in the caverns, we were given an armload of damp, moldy weeds. We were allowed a small fire in the cages, for cooking, and to ward off the dampness. We took these subterranean ferns, mosses, and mushrooms, and brewed them into a stew. Once, we were given a dark, almost black, type of mushroom that produced hallucinations.

I must have been a captive of these terrible devil-men for two weeks, perhaps a month, when the gray men appeared from out of the tunnels. The devils scrambled in the opposite direction, grunting with fright, as the gray men shot them with gas guns. Several of the bestial men-animals were killed. Prisoners were released from the cage, given a toga-like robe for clothing, and taken through the tunnels for medical attention. They had a strange sort of vehicle, not like our automobiles, that was parked in the tunnels.

A physician led us into a mobile laboratory. The room had large number of machines and, even under the lights, the metal was grayish in color. Everything was made of this metal and even their clothing appeared to be metallic. I retained a sense of where I was, but the leader of the group indicated to the doctor that I should be treated.

They spoke perfect French, but with a strange accent. 'Your mind is disturbed because of your experience,' said the leader of the group. He was about five feet tall, muscular, with only his face visible under the helmet of the same gray metal. His face was more elongated, thinner, than those of the human beings I have met. It was gray in color, almost like the cast of old baking dough.

We were taken individually into another vehicle that looked like a combination hospital and computer room. Another man, who seemed to be a physician, indicated I should lay back on a table made from the same grayish metal. He also spoke in French, indicating that the treatment would not hurt me.

'You will feel no pain,' he said. 'We have tried to erase memories from the mind but they are never totally gone. They will come forth through dreams, nightmares, and disguised thoughts. We are attaching you to a machine that provides you with information on why you were tortured by the animal men.'

'Can't you tell me,' I inquired.

'It would take many years of time, as you measure it,' he replied. 'The machines implant information in your mind without error. The data is not filtered through my mind, but remains purified.'

After the treatment, I was taken to another section of the tunnels. Some of the men in metallic uniforms were sealing off the tunnels. The leader designated a man to lead me back to the surface world, and in another two hours, we were in the sewers of Paris. I was back on the streets in a short while. I must have looked very strange, walking barefoot through the streets in winter. A gendarme stopped me and I was taken into custody and, eventually, my family was contacted. I spent many weeks in a mental hospital and, today, I am in a sanitarium trying to recover from the experience . . .

What was the message given to the young woman through the machine?

Many millions of years ago, she related, the earth was devoid of human life The 'starmen' selected our planet as a space laboratory, transplanting various types of people from different planets onto our earth. *Homo sapiens* became the dominant species as our aggressive, war-like characteristics drove the other species from us. Some of these species became extinct. Others vanished and even the 'starmen' don't know what occurred. They simply disappeared without a trace.

As the human race continued to grow, some species were driven underground to the caverns for their survival. They adapted themselves to the life beneath the surface and, in time, they created the tunnels and cavern cities. There were tremendous problems related to biological mutations and the necessary evolution of the species to survive the environment of the inner earth. In time, the original colonists degenerated into the brutal, horrible animal men. In ancient times, these degenerates preyed upon surface humanity through raids on outlying areas. Ancient stories of strange appearances of unusual animals, werewolves, and men-beasts are memories of battles between our ancestors and the animal men.

Eventually, mankind developed weaponry to defend themselves. The men-beasts were pushed back under the ground. They now prowl only at night and they're very careful to avoid detection by humans. The wars, the atomic age, and evolution of the animal-men, has created the problem today. The animal-men are a great threat to human survival. The animal-men have evolved into a deadly species, more crafty and extremely cunning. The constant tests of nuclear weapons have destroyed, or cracked, many of the great tunnels. Whole cavern cities have been wiped out by these tests. The animal-men are growing stronger. They've become the heirs to advanced weaponry, airships, and electromagnetic weaponry The animal-men are on the march to conquer the entire planet, including the surface world.

Who were the men in metallic uniforms?

They are what we would call a biological team from the far reaches of space. During a routine check of the earth, they learned of the mutations that had occurred among the animal-men. They brought back their instruments and established several 'breeding stations,' notably under the oceans and seas. They plan to observe the war between the animal-men and the armies of our surface nations.

Will they save us from these demonic creatures?

Our salvation will come through our own efforts. The 'starmen' are observers of the battle between the species on this planet. They have no plans to disturb the functions of natural selection by committing their weaponry to either species.

According to this theory, we didn't evolve from the apes. Is that correct?

To the contrary, the apes evolved downward from us as a degenerated species of early *homo sapiens*. It is as if the surface world produced a similar group of animal-men.

Should we believe this story?

The lady approached our representatives in Paris last year, seeking more data on the hollow earth. She believed the Hollow Earth Society might provide more information to put her terrible experience into some sort of understanding. Unfortunately, we do not have the funds to maintain a library except at our headquarters. Our man in Paris checked her history and background in great detail. She disappeared for about four months, at the time indicated. He checked the elevator at the office building where her kidnapping allegedly took place. The shaft ended at the basement but – strangely enough – there were signs of fresh masonry construction at the bottom of the elevator shaft. We asked for permission to test the shaft for a possible proof of her story. The building owners refused to allow tests of any type.

How does her story check with the Shaver information?

Shaver stated that people on the surface evolved from the abandonero. He reported our ancestors were those ancient people who were unable to gain entry into the caves. As they roamed the radiated surface of our world, they were reduced to a species known as the Neanderthal man. Those that did not die off eventually built up an immunity to the radiation rays of the sun.

As time progressed, humanity forgot about the ancestral catastrophe except for the folklore about vanished civilizations like Atlantis and Lemuria, and memory of a group known as the 'Masters.'

Organized, pseudo-scientific investigation of the Hollow

Earth Mystery has been the goal of the Hollow Earth Society since it was established in England in 1961. The group has been unconcerned about the reality of their beliefs, placing their strongest emphasis on gaining new converts to their cause. The current president of the organization is Albert McDonald, a Welsh-born businessman with a missionary gleam in his eyes. He has a zealous ability to convince almost anyone of the far-out beliefs of his organization.

McDonald's Hollow Earth Society is admittedly a small organization with 432 members on a world-wide basis. 'We remain very effective for a small group,' he announced, during an interview in his London apartment. 'We are represented with members in 32 countries and, hopefully, we can generate enough energy for a world convention in the next three years.'

What are the goals of his organization? 'We want to send an expedition down into the interior of the earth,' McDonald replied. 'We must check out the stories of cavern cities, underground passageways, and vast tunnels that connect the continents. If there is any truth to these tales, then surface people are endangered by the beings who live in the interior.'

As I sat in McDonald's apartment on the outskirts of London, I envisioned the day when a U.S. Senator would speak up in behalf of such an expedition. I could almost imagine the time when presidents, dictators, and kings, waited anxiously at the entrance of some underground tunnel for news from the official Hollow Earth Expedition. It seemed unreal, too much like a sequence from a science-fiction movie where some terrible beast tries to devour our planet.

'You can't be serious?' I looked over at my bearded, dark-eyed host. 'If the world was hollow then we would have known about it long before now.'

'Explain the stories of mysterious visits from unknown beings throughout history,' McDonald snapped. 'What about the legends, folklore, and myths? How can you explain such creatures as the Abominable Snowmen, except if they're from a cavern city? What about sea serpents, the Loch Ness monsters, people who disappear?'

'I admit there are many unexplained mysteries in the world,' I agreed. 'But they can't be lumped into a neat little file tagged as "Hollow Earth – All Mysteries Explained." That's wishful thinking. There's not a single shred of evidence to indicate that our planet is hollow. There's plenty of scientific evidence to indicate that the earth is exactly the way our scientists say it is.'

'Don't you believe in the inner lands and the Masters?'

'Not until they send someone around to help me write my manuscripts.'

'Perhaps we need people who don't believe,' McDonald admitted. 'Look what happened to Germany when the true believers took over.'

Cavity cities . . . subterranean supermen . . . utopian societies . . . wild men-beasts . . . demonic deros . . . *Vril* power . . . The King of the World in the Cave of the Ancients . . . tunnels and UFOs from the inner earth. The hollow earth mystery contains something for everyone and this may partially explain the popularity of this occult belief. Do you enjoy tales of horror in the style of Lovecraft or Poe? The deros surpass many fictional monsters in sheer horror and many people claim the deros are real – not fictitious creatures. Gottfried Messerschmidt, a German expert on the occult, traveled throughout the world collecting incidents of alleged encounters with beings from the inner earth. The result was a remarkable volume known as 'The Messerschmidt Manuscript,' a frightening collection of horror and terror beneath the earth. The French woman's experiences in the last chapter were taken from that manuscript, one of many people who claim to have stumbled or been kidnapped into the hollow earth.

People who enjoy philosophical, religious, mathematical, or scientific puzzles are lured by the legends of these vast subterranean civilizations. Perhaps Atlantis was real and Lemuria did exist as a great continent in the Pacific Ocean. Could Shaver's Atlans or Titans have sought shelter in the caverns? Ar they waiting below, hoping that man can save himself and solve his own problems, yet ready to make a messianic march to the surface at a critical moment?

Throughout history, an unusual group of scientists, eccentrics, and plain ordinary crackpots have dabbled with these intriguing questions. Plato wrote about 'enormous subterranean streams' and 'tunnels, both broad and narrow, in the interior of the earth.' Plato and his contemporaries in ancient Greece were fervent believers in an under world. He wrote:

'. . . He is the god who sits in the center, on the navel of the earth; and he is the interpreter of religion to all mankind.' Students of antiquity have often found the strange phrase, '. . . the navel of the earth,' in ancient literature. The phrase was used by people who presumably had no contact with each other during ancient times.

In 1682, the reknowned Dr. Edmund Halley gazed up into the night skies and saw the comet that was named for him. Ten years later, in 1692, Dr. Halley was Astronomer Royal for England. From his official role as the king's astronomer, Dr. Halley spoke before the Royal Society of London and his remarks were published as an essay.

'Beneath the crust of the earth, which is 500 miles thick, is a hollow void,' said the noted astronomer. 'Inside this space are three planets. They are approximately the size of Mars, Venus, and Mercury.'

The theory was adopted by Leonard Euler (1707–1783), the noted Swiss mathematician, and one of the founders of higher mathematics. The Eulerian equation and Euler's formula are named after him; he is known for his work in calculus, trigonometry, and analytic mathematics. 'Euler decided that there was not three planets in the hollow earth, as Halley declared,' said Gunther Rosenberg. 'Euler felt that there was a central sun inside the earth's interior, which provided daylight to a splendid subterranean civilization.'

The Hollow Earth has been an American belief since the Pilgrims first stepped ashore in New England. Cotton Mather, a prominent New England clergyman and political figure, wrote in 1721 of an interior land in his book, *The Christian Philosopher*. The hypothesis lay dormant for a few years until Sir John Leslie, a Scottish physicist and mathematician, speculated on what might lie beneath our feet. Well-known for his work in radiation, Leslie decided that there were two fiery suns inside the earth. He named these two planets, Pluto and Proserpina.

The next believer was one of the most unusual men in American history. Captain John Cleves Symmes, who was given several medals for bravery during the War of 1812, led a band of Commandos against the British at Fort Erie, Canada, over-ran the redcoat defenses, and became a hero. Captain John Cleves Symmes was an aggressive, highly individualistic officer. His quick temper and sharp tongue had lashed many of his soldiers and a handful of his superior officers. After the war ended, he was assigned to an isolated U.S. Army fort on the upper Mississippi river.

'It's going to be lonely up there, but I expect I'll stay out of trouble,' Symmes told a fellow officer.

'How are you going to spend the time?' asked his friend.

'I'm taking two trunks of books with me,' Symmes said. 'This tour of duty is a blessing. I'll have a couple of years to catch up on my reading.'

Symmes had developed in interest in science; he was extremely fascinated by the various schools of speculation on how the earth was formed. During his time at the fort, Symmes made a detailed study of the works of Professor Abner Burnett. Burnett theorized that our planet had once been a small mudball covered with oil. As this core floated through space, it picked up space garbage to form the earth's crust.

A Professor Woodward was another of Symmes' favorites. Woodward believed the earth was composed of distinct layers of strata 'like the coats of an onion.' Other eighteenth century scientists thought the earth originated as a comet. A liquid center had formed in the comet, which had then been covered by the earth's crust. 'In other words, the earth was formed like an egg,' remarked Gunther Rosenberg.

Symmes read these various hypotheses and then created his own conception of planetary origin. 'The earth is like the planets beyond us,' he explained to a patient group of fellow officers. 'There are rings around the planet of Saturn, so this establishes the principle of concentric spheres. Our earth, and the other planets, are hollow.'

'What's in the inside?' asked a curious lieutenant.

'There are five concentric spheres inside the outer surface,'

Symmes reported. 'This is like five globes placed one inside the other. They have a common center.'

'But what about Newton's theory of gravity?'

'Newton was completely wrong,' said the captain. 'The atmosphere of the world is filled with an invisible substance. I call this an aerial elastic fluid. It is composed of tiny spheres of ether that are hollow. This invisible substance pushes down against the earth instead of the Newton theory of a *pulling* process.' Having dismissed Newton's theory of gravity, Symmes decided that since his ether spheres were hollow, it was because 'a nebular mass in rotation, as our earth during formation, will not assume the form of a solid sphere, but rather of a hollow one.'

'That seems a little hard to believe,' said an enlisted man, quickly adding a loud 'sir!'

'Not at all, sergeant,' replied Symmes. 'Everything in nature is hollow. We had buffalo meat for mess tonight. Did you notice the bones? They are hollow. Look at the reeds that grow along the riverbank. They're hollow. The hollow object is nature's way of saving material.'

After a few more minutes of discussion, Captain Symmes left his astonished audience and turned in for the night. His listeners drifted off and, as the fort settled down for the night, the lieutenant and the sergeant were left to ponder Symmes' theory.

The sergeant scratched a line in the dirt with a hollow reed. 'What do you think, lieutenant?' he asked.

'Maybe the old man is right. I don't know, do you?'

'Yep. He's right. Some things are hollow,' said the sergeant. He pointed toward a cluster of large rocks that lay downriver from the fort. 'But, lieutenant, rocks ain't hollow. Rocks are as soid as anything on earth. I think the captain, excusing the expression, has got rocks in his head.'

Symmes' zealous sermons about the hollow earth were a regular event after the evening meal. Officers and enlisted men under his command listened respectfully, stifling their boredom. When Captain Symmes retired for the night, they gathered in small groups and discussed his sanity. 'He's a dang good quartermaster but he sure sounds like a preacher trying to convert sinners,' declared the sergeant.

Captain Symmes remained at the fort for four years. He resigned his commission in 1816. 'It is time to prove my theories,' he declared to his weary audience. 'I'll go down river by flat-boat to St. Louis. I'm going to establish a trading post there and, from those funds of commerce, I will launch en expedition to the inner earth.'

In the spring of 1816, Captain John Cleves Symmes, late of the U.S. Army, obtained a government permit and established a trading post. He sold supplies to traders, mountain men, and explorers. Within a few weeks he met, and married, a charming widow with six children. He fathered four more children from his marriage. Despite his new business, and the expanding demand of his family life, Symmes continued to dig through books to substantiate his hollow earth belief.

Symmes finally decided that there were holes at the poles; he was the first man to theorize in this aspect of the mystery. 'A man could lead an expedition down into those five planets inside our earth,' he claimed. 'I can sit here until old age takes me. I'm going to publish a circular and mail it to the colleges, universities, our president and the Congress.'

In May, 1818, prominent people in several countries received this circular:

St. Louis,
Missouri Territory
North America

Light Gives Light To Light
Discover Ad infinitum

I declare that the earth is hollow, habitable within; containing a number of solid concentrick spheres; one within the other, and it is open at the poles twelve or sixteen degrees. I pledge my life in support of this truth, and am ready to explore the hollow if the world will support and aid me in the undertaking.

I have ready for the press a treatise in the principles of Matter, wherein I show proofs of the above propositions, account for various phenomena, and disclose Dr. Darwin's 'Golden Secret.'

My terms are the patronage of this and the new world. I dedicate to my wife and her ten children.

I select Dr. S. L. Mitchel, Sir H. Davy and Baron Alexander Von Humboldt as my protectors. I ask one hundred brave companions, well equipped to start from Siberia, on the fall season, with reindeer and sledges, on the ice of the frozen sea; I engage we will find a warm and rich land, stocked with thrifty vegetables and animals; if not men, on reaching one degree northward of latitude 82; we will return in the succeeding spring.

John Cleves Symmes of Ohio
Late Captain of Infantry

Before Symmes mailed his circular, he added another sheet. It was signed by several prominent physicians and businessmen in St. Louis territory; it testified that Captain Symmes was a good father, respected businessman, and a Christian gentleman. '. . . He is considered sane by all who know him,' the statement concluded.

His mailing completed, Captain Symmes tended to his trading post and awaited reaction from the world. Scientists in England, Italy, and America adopted a 'wait-and-see' indifference to his project. Symmes' *Theory of Concentric Spheres* was accepted with wild enthusiasm in Russia; the Czar was obsessed with the idea of polar openings, new lands, and five interior planets to be explored. In France, the scientific establishment rolled their collective eyes and questioned Symmes' sanity. '. . . we wouldn't request a single franc for such an outlandish proposal,' a member of the French academy informed reporters.

While the scientists waited, the public became enthusiastic about Symmes' theory. Within a short time, Captain Symmes, his wife, and their ten children, closed down the trading post. They left St. Louis territory and moved to Newport, Kentucky. Symmes wrote articles for newspapers; one of the first to be published was 'Light Between the Spheres' in an August, 1819, edition of the *Cincinatti National Intelligencer*.

The energetic Captain also hit the lecture trail, hoping to drum up funds for his expedition. ''We're never going to explore those inner lands unless we have funds,' Symmes exhorted his audiences. 'Write your Senators and Congressmen to petition the U.S. government for funds to place Old Glory on those interior planets.'

Symmes found an eager audience among the small towns of frontier America. There were no fees charged to attend his lectures and hundreds of people flocked to hear and see the man with funny ideas. Symmes was quick-tempered, erudite, and impatient. In Kentucky, he tossed a coughing listener bodily out of the lecture hall. In Indiana, he cuffed a skeptical farmer across the ears and then 'soundly thrashed the impertinent fellow.' Either by word or fist, Symmes spread his gospel.

Gradually, Symmes organized a band of disciples who believed with him. One of the most prominent was James McBride, a millionaire from Miami, Ohio. McBride, who owned an imposing personal library, was a trustee of Miami University and the owner of a large lecture hall. Inspired by the thoughts of Symmes' inner lands, McBride convinced the zealous Captain to move to Hamilton, Ohio. 'I'll work with you,' McBride said. 'Consider me your patron and assitant. I have influence and know how to get a petition before Congress.'

McBride contacted Representative Richard M. Johnson of Kentucky, a skilled politician who would later become vice president of the United States. In January, 1823, Rep. Johnson stood up on the floor of Congress. 'I repectfully submit a petition to this learned body,' said Rep. Johnson, 'that the

U.S. Government finance an expedition to claim the lands inside the earth.'

'What did he say?' An elderly Congressman from New York twirled his ear trumpet in dismay.

A younger Congressman leaned over to his elderly companion. 'Dick Johnson wants us to finance a group of men to explore the center of the earth.'

The aged Congressman stopped rapping his ear trumpet on his desk. 'That's what I thought he said,' he mumbled. 'But, I assumed there was dust or something in my hearing aid.'

Despite the skeptical attitude of his fellow lawmakers, Rep. Johnson forcefully pressed the petition. Simultaneously, several hundred letters poured into Washington from Ohio, Kentucky, Indiana, and Missouri Territoy. 'There are sane, intelligent voters demanding that we bring great honor and profit to the United States by opening up these new lands,' announced Rep. Johnson.

'I move to table this petition,' snapped a Congressman from Pennsylvania.

'Let's do anything but shelve the proposal,' pleaded Rep. Johnson. 'Something useful may happen if we send out an expedition.'

Despite his dramatic pleas, Congress ignored the petition from Rep. Johnson and the petition to send a Symmes expedition into the subterranean worlds died. Congress then got back to the business of ratifying President Monroe's Doctrine.

Lesser men would have accepted defeat. Captain Symmes stepped up his lecture engagements, redoubled his output of articles, and worked every day of the week to convince a skeptical world.

'Isn't it about time to write a book on your theory?' inquired his patron, James McBride.

'I don't have the time,' replied Symmes. 'Why don't you take my notes and put them into book form?'

James McBride published a small volume entitled *Symmes' Theory of Concentric Spheres* (Morgan, Lodge & Gisher; Cincinnati; 1826). He wrote:

> According to Captain Symmes, the planet which has been designated the Earth, is composed of at least five hollow concentric spheres, with spaces between each, an atmosphere surrounding each; and habitable as well upon the concave as the convex surface. Each of these spheres are widely open at their poles . . . Although the particular location of the places where the verges of the polar openings are believed to exist, may not have been ascertained with absolute certainty, yet they are believed to be nearly correct; their localities have been ascertained from appearances that exist in these regions: such as a belt or zone surrounding the globe where trees and other vegetation (except moss; do not grow; the tides of the ocean flowing in different directions, and appearing to meet; the existence of volcanoes; the *ground swells* in the sea being more frequent; the *Aurora Borealis* appearing to the southward (and others) . . .

John Symmes was touring Canada on a nation-wide lecture tour in the winter of 1828 when he became extremely ill. His sons rushed to Canada and brought their father back to his home in Hamilton, Ohio. He died there in his sleep on May 29, 1829. He was forty-nine years old. If you're passing through Hamilton, Ohio, sometime you might want to stop and see the monument that was erected there by his son, Americus Vespucius Symmes, in the replica of a hollow globe above a stone shaft. The inscription reads: '. . . Captain John Cleves Symmes was a Philosopher, and the originator of "Symmes Theory of Concentric Spheres and Polar voids." He contended the Earth was hollow and habitable within.'

Symmes had gathered a strange band of believers to his hollow banners. Some were visionaries with a fanatical gleam in their eyes. Others were weary men and women who hoped to retire permanently to a gentle civilization within the interior. A few were plain, ordinary fortune hunters, hungry adventurers, or soldiers of fortune. Like his theory, Symmes' disciples were a few steps outside of the norm.

One of the most unusual of this odd lot was a fast-talking young man, Joseph Reynolds, who graduated from Ohio University. Equipped with a sharp mind and a cheater's morals, Reynolds had slipped through college; he had learned to love fast horses and faster women. Instead of post-graduate study, Reynolds decided to do a little research in the fast buck department.

Joe Reynolds was searching for a sure thing to trim the populace when he wandered into a lecture hall one evening. He blinked a few times when Captain Symmes swore the earth was hollow. Reynolds suppressed his laughter when he noticed the audience was awed by the captain's speech. When an overflowing collection plate passed through the house, Reynolds decided he had stumbled into a good thing.

Acting like an awed college sophomore, Reynolds approached Captain Symmes. 'I am an educated man,' he announced. 'Henceforth, I will devote my life, my talents, and my energy to support your cause.'

Captain Symmes had met all kinds of boobs along the lecture trail. 'What can you do, sir?' he inquired.

'Whatever you wish,' Reynolds said, smoothly. 'I have an independent income so there is no need for a salary. I just want the opportunity to serve you.'

Captain Symmes welcomed the newcomer to the flock and, within a week, Reynolds knew he was on the track of big money. He worked tirelessly as an advance man for the captain. He rented lecture halls, conned newsmen for articles on forthcoming lectures, and hired shills to talk up the lecture when the captain hit town. Although the lecture halls were jammed and crowded, the most interested spectator was Joseph Reynolds.

Reynolds slumped down in a front-row seat each night and listened rapturously to the captain's lecture. As the hollow earth messiah talked, he was pleased to see his protege scribbling down his every word. Sometimes, after a lecture, Reynolds asked Symmes to explain an obscure point.

'I hate to bother you so much,' Reynolds apologized. He smiled shyly at the captain.

Symmes slapped the young man on the back. 'Don't think anything of it,' he said. 'I like to see someone with intelligence take an interest in my work.'

Following several months of beating the drums for Captain Symmes, Reynolds had filled the lecture halls in Pennsylvania, Maine, New York, and Connecticut. When Symmes mentioned going to Canada to build up support, Reynolds knew it was time to bow out. His funds were running low. Symmes had also complained about his protege's interest in buxom young ladies in the audience.

'My aunt is seriously ill,' lied Reynolds. 'I'll catch up with you in Canada.'

As Symmes crossed the border on his last lecture tour, Joseph Reynolds headed for New York and walked brashly into the offices of a booking agent. 'I am a scientist who has just returned from an extended journey into the hollow earth,' Reynolds announced.

'And,' snapped the agent, 'I am the king of Prussia.'

'Can you handle bookings for me,' asked Reynolds.

'You mean to say you're willing to tell people about it?'

Reynolds looked firmly at the booking agent, a bald, round little man. 'For a substantial fee and a crowded lecture hall.'

'Will people believe it?' the agent asked.

'Captain Symmes of Ohio is doing good with this bit,' Reynolds said. 'I can give a better lecture than he can and, if you want to agent the deal, you get half of the money.'

The agent thought over Reynolds' proposition for two seconds, then, his reply throbbed with enthusiasm. 'God has sent you here,' he intoned. 'I've had dozens of inquiries about someone to speak on the Symmes theory. Let's get moving.'

Within a couple of weeks, Joseph Reynolds was standing on a lecture platform in Washington D.C. and exciting an audience with his tall tales. It had taken a few days to get his speech into shape. The work had been worth it because the audience was spell-bound by his stories of vast subterranean cities, new lands, inner suns, and twenty-foot-giants who guarded a subterranean treasure.

'It is there for the taking,' he cried. 'We have to place that great flag of the United States over the lands within the earth. The United States can become the greatest nation on the surface of the world. We can rule these inner lands, commence trade with the inhabitants, and open up five planets for new frontiers.'

When his speech was over, the audience dug deep and filled the collection plate. Reynolds and his agent were busily stuffing money into their pockets, when a man with a distinguished manner walked up. The stranger slapped Reynolds on the back. 'I'm going to help you,' the newcomer announced.

Reynolds eyed the money he had collected and remembered how he had gotten into the lecture field. He didn't want anyone cutting in on a good thing. He didn't plan on spending any time with the yokels.

'I'm busy,' he said, counting off the night's take.

'I am Samuel L. Southard,' said the stranger. 'I am the Secretary of the Navy.'

Reynolds stopped flipping through his currency.

'For the United States government?' he inquired. His eyes sparkled with integrity.

The Secretary of the Navy explained that he was interested in launching an expedition to the inner earth. 'I suggest that you lead the U.S. Navy to these lands,' Southard said. 'It would be a boon for the United States.'

Within a few days, Reynolds agreed and thought about his personal boon. Southard had convinced President John Quincy Adams that Symmes' hypothesis should be investigated. President Adams listened intently to the plan then ordered a naval ship to be supplied and outfitted for a voyage to the South Pole. Before the Naval expedition could be launched, President Adams lost his residence at the White House. Andrew Jackson, the practical-minded politician from Tennessee, was installed as president. 'Old Hickory' wasn't buying anything connected with the hollow earth.

Meanwhile, Joseph Reynolds continued to pull in the crowds with his imaginative lectures. Symmes had died and Reynolds was now the spokesman for the whole hollow earth crowd. Reynolds was content to make his speeches, count the money, and enjoy the good life. Unlike Symmes, Reynolds found that every crowd included someone who wanted to finance a journey to the interior.

'I am getting tired of these yokels wanting to see the giants,' Reynolds snapped to his agent. 'We got a good deal here. You keep these boobs off my back.'

The agent looked off in the distance. 'What would it cost to outfit an expedition?'

Reynolds shook his head. 'Too much.'

'What would ten percent of that be?' asked the agent.

'A lot of money,' Reynolds declared. 'A whole lot of money.'

'Just think,' continued the agent, 'that an expedition might be formed with stockholders who would profit on anything found inside the earth.'

Reynolds listened as the wheels started turning in his mind.

'We skim ten or twenty percent off the top,' the little agent outlined. 'You lead the expedition as the head scientist. The voyage will fail – but, we'll both be rich.'

'Yup,' said Reynolds. 'A whole lot of money.'

A company was established and impressive stock certificates printed. A shady financial operator peddled the certificates in the hollow earth expedition. Wealthy men in New York began to talk about the hollow earth as the glamour stock of that era. Whispers, rumors, and outright lies were encouraged by the nervy band of manipulators. Finally, enough people believed in concentric circles and inner planets to finance the expedition. It was late October, 1829, when Captain N. B. Palmer stood on the deck of the brig, *Annawan*, as the craft sailed from New York harbor. Captain Robert Pendleton commanded the brig, *Seraph*, that followed behind. The two ships set course for the South Pole and the land beyond the known world.

The senior scientist and man-in-charge of the expedition was supposed to be J. Reynolds, who had packed several cases of rare booze for the voyage. He planned to stay in his cabin and practice alcoholic alchemy. 'Good luck,' the agent had said before the ships sailed. 'I'll watch over things here at home. Have a good vacation.'

Reports that filtered back to New York were vague, contradictory, and none agreed on what occurred on the expedition. One account was that the two ships pulled into a south sea isle and spent a few months there, with Reynolds and the crew cavorting with the native girls. Another account claimed the ships reached the South polar continent at latitude 82 degrees and sent a group out over the polar ice cap. The sailors became lost and almost starved to death before they were rescued.

'We believe that the expedition was aborted by a rebellion by a mutinous crew,' said Gunther Rosenberg, president and founder of the European Occult Research Society. 'Several accounts claimed the crewmen mutinied off the coast of Chile. Reynolds and the ships' officers were put ashore. The crewmen took off on a pirates' foray. Every account agrees that the expedition failed to find the south polar opening.'

What happened to fast-talking Joseph Reynolds?

'One account says the J. Reynolds aboard the ship was a scientist named John Reynolds,' Rosenberg stated. 'I tend to believe that Reynolds remained in New York with his money. If he was put ashore in Chile, he may have died there. He just dropped out of sight after the expedition sailed.'

Symmes and his followers had created enough interest in the hollow earth to trigger the imagination of writers all over the world. During the 1820's, a New York publishing house cashed in on the fad by printing *Symzonia: a Voyage of Discovery* (J. Seymour; New York; 1823). The book was purportedly written by the pseudonymous Captain Adam Seaborn. The fictional novel was a satire on the entire hollow earth movement. 'Captain Seaborn tells of outfitting an expedition to the hollow earth,' said Gunther Rosenberg. 'Near the polar hole, the crew discovered the bones of a monster and the captain allowed his ship to be sucked into a powerful current from the inner world. They find a new continent and name it Symzonia, a take-off on Symmes and his theories.'

In Symzonia, the captain and his crew make their way to an enchanted metropolis populated by a race of albino humans. The inhabitants speak a whistling, musical language and wear snow-white garments to indicate their purity. The inner earth is illuminated by a couple of suns and moons, which light a socialistic form of utopian government. Their benign ruler was known simply as 'The Best Man.' The Symzonians possessed enormous sums of gold, advanced weaponry, and a desire to keep their secrets free from contamination by surface *homo sapiens*. Captain Seaborn and his crew are driven from Symzonia and forced back into the greedy outer world.

In the 1830s, Edgar Allan Poe based three of his short stories on Symmes' theory. 'Ms. Found in a Bottle' related the tragedy of a large ocean vessel grabbed by the strong currents of a swirling whirlpool at the South Pole. '. . . We are plunging madly within the grasp of the whirlpool – and amid a roaring, and bellowing, and thundering of ocean and tempest, the ship is quivering,' Poe concluded. '—Oh God! and – going down!' Poe's other hollow earth stories were

The Unparalleled Adventure of One Hans Pfall, and *The Narrative of A. Gordon Pym.*

Jules Verne's popular novel *Journey to the Center of the Earth* combined the hollow earth ideas of Captain Symmes and Sir John Leslie. Professor W. F. Lyons published *A Hollow Globe* in 1868, but failed to mention Symmes as the man who had triggered the hullabaloo. Angered by this ommission of his father's name, Americus Vespucius compiled his father's notes and published *The Symmes Theory of Concentric Spheres, Demonstrating That the Earth is Hollow, Habitable Within, and Widely Open About the Poles* (Bradley & Gilbert; Louisville; 1878). Americus declared that he was merely the editor of the book; his father was given full credit for authorship. However, the son could not resist a thought or two on the inhabitants of the inner world. 'They are the Ten Lost Tribes of Israel,' Americus informed newsmen. 'Reason, common sense, and all the analogies in the natural universe conspire to support and establish the theory of a hollow earth.'

Captain John Cleves Symmes, an eccentric individual by any standard, left a considerable legacy to the world. His theories resulted in imaginative works by Edgar Allan Poe and Jules Verne. He was the prime mover in weaving a magical spell around a theory of subterranean worlds that has continued to this day. Most of Symmes' followers believed in him to their dying day.

COOK AND PEARY: THE NORTH POLE CONTROVERSY

The sun was setting on the rich, black earth around Aurora, Illinois, when a burly, dark-mustachioed man walked through the swinging doors of a neighborhood salon. Flashing his usual broad smile at the bartender, Marshall B. Gardner crawled upon a stool and waited for his usual stein of beer.

'I liked that chapter about the North Pole,' said the bartender. He pushed a frosty mug of beer toward Gardner. 'You figured that Peary and Cook were both wrong.'

'They had to be,' Gardner replied, complacently. 'You can't find something that doesn't exist.'

The bartender nodded in agreement. 'Well, it's an entirely new idea.'

'Our planet has holes at the poles,' Gardner continued, 'so with the earth being hollow, Peary and Cook couldn't have reached the North Pole.'

A stranger in the saloon cleared his throat. 'I'm a salesman just passing through,' he said, 'and I couldn't help hearing what you said. You really believe the earth is hollow?'

'Certainly.' Gardner sipped his beer. 'A study of the information can lead only to that conclusion.'

'This is Marshall Gardner,' the bartender waved toward his tall, stout customer. 'Mr. Gardner is a very respected man in Aurora.'

'Are you a scientist?' asked the salesman.

'I work in the corset factory as a maintenance man.'

The stranger smiled, smugly. 'Then, you're not an expert on the subject?'

'He's a real expert,' the bartender said, quickly. 'Mr. Gardner is author of the book *A Journey To The Earth's Interior*:

Or, Have The Poles Really Been Discovered? That's an autographed copy over there behind the glass case.'

'But, you're not a scientist,' the salesman persisted.

'And I wouldn't want to be,' Gardner replied. 'They're fuzzy thinkers. Nasmyth and Carpenter in their book, *The Moon Considered as a Planet, a World, and a Satellite* wrote a standard work on the subject. They said that the light reflected from the moon indicated that there was no atmosphere on the moon's surface. They said the moon's atmosphere was two thousand times thinner than our own. If there is no air on the moon, they theorized, then there can be no water.'

'Why not?' asked the salesman.

'If there was water, it would vaporize and produce an atmosphere of water vapor,' Gardner said. 'Do you agree?'

The salesman blinked and nodded.

'Recently, Professor William J. Pickering of Harvard University made a study of the moon from his observatory in Jamaica,' Gardner related. 'He declared the canal lines on the moon were artificial. He also asserted there is a race of superior beings living up there. Did you read his report?'

'I'm afraid not,' the salesman said, meekly.

'Well, if there is no air or water on the moon, how does this race of superior people do their gardening?' asked Gardner. 'They would certainly have to be a superior race. Very superior. Perhaps we should get a few of them down here on Earth.'

'Why?'

Gardner chuckled. 'They could raise watermelons in the Sahara desert. But, perhaps it is only artificial flowers that they grow along the waterless canals in a land where vegetation is never hurt by storms because there isn't any air to create winds.'

Although he had a limited, little-red-schoolhouse education, Marshall B. Gardner proved to be a strong researcher who could find the flaws in many scientific pronouncements. His book was originally published in 1913 at the author's expense. Gardner declared that the turmoil leading up to World War I diverted public attention from his theory. He published another edition in 1920 that contained numerous drawings and diagrams. 'Some people have said that they would consider our theory triumphant if it were not for the fact that the North Pole had actually been discovered,' he declared. From there, he went on to consider the details of the controversy that swirled around Cook and Peary, who claimed to have discovered the North Pole. Gardner wrote:

The first claim to the Pole

> The first claim, of course, was made by Dr. Frederick A. Cook, who announced that he had reached the North Pole on April 21, 1908. Then, within a few days of his announcement and the general acceptance of Cook's claim by the world – although there were a few dissenting voices – there came a dispatch from Peary to the effect that he had discovered the Pole, reaching it, as he claimed, on April 6, 1909, nearly a year after Cook's alleged discovery.
>
> As Cook was the first to make the claim we will consider his claim first, noting, however, the ... difficulties in making proper observations, due to the fact the sun was only a few degrees above the horizon. This applied to Peary as well as to Cook. Both were in a position where it was impossible to make very accurate observations.

Peary's Rivalry

> The general acceptance of Cook's claim was based on his prediction that he could establish by field notes and mathematical observations the truth of his claim. But on one excuse or another he never did produce all the notes he said he would. He claimed that Peary caused some of his data to be buried, which may be true. But at any rate it was not long before the first faith in Cook was suc-

ceeded by a very general skepticism. This skepticism may have been started by Peary's denial of Cook's claim, a denial which was made promptly and vigorously in no uncertain or diplomatic language. But it was undoubtedly fed by Cook's own policy of not giving the world proper scientific data. In fact Peary's sharp way of criticising Cook and the facts which soon came out tending to show that Peary thought he owned the polar regions and the Eskimos, and that he had taken some of the stores which Cook had cached pending his return from the north – all that created a great prejudice against Peary, and Cook seemed to have things his own way. But he never submitted real proofs.

Melville is skeptical

And his dispatches about the pole did not sound convincing to men who knew the conditions in the north. Rear-Admiral Melville, of the United States Navy, himself an old time arctic exlorer said in an interview:

'It was the crazy dispatches purporting to have come from Dr. Cook about the conditions he found there, and other things, that caused a doubt in my mind about Cook's having found the pole.'

The London *Daily Mail* said:

'The long message in which Cook recounted his journey was by general consent pronounced unconvincing, and the further particulars which he communicated since landing at Copenhagen have not removed all ground for doubt ... A large section of the public still entertains doubts and asks why it is he has not brought with him his journal and detailed observations to establish the truth of his statements.'

Tittman's remarks lead directly to our theory

Dr. George Tittman, head of the coast and geodetic survey at Washington was asked if Cook's claim to have been at the pole could be checked up by comparing it with what scientists knew would be the conditions at that spot. His answer was in itself almost an admission that the time was ripe for our own theory to be given to the world. For what he did was to acknowledge the bankruptcy of science when it came to having knowledge of that region. He said:

'There are really no scientific theories as to what is immediately around the pole. There are some theorists who think that there is an open sea and some who think that a fertile spot is there. Scientific men are inclined to think that there may be little difference in immediate conditions close to the pole from those in the Arctic regions miles from there.'

That is really a remarkable admission from a scientist. For, if the orthodox scientific idea about the polar regions is right, it ought to be colder there than anywhere else. And yet Dr. Tittman admits that practically all scientists agree that this is not the fact. Some, he says, think there is an open sea there and others say there is fertile land. We can see why some of them think there is open sea there because, as we have already seen, all explorers who have gone far enough north have found an open sea. But why should any scientists think there is fertile land at the pole? It seems impossible on their own theories of a solid earth with increasing cold as you go north. Even if the cold at the poles was not enough to freeze the sea up, how could it be warm enough to produce fertility? The answer is, that the scientists who say that are simply men who are honest enough to follow all the evidence. They have seen the evidence already cited in this book of animal life and vegetation in the north, but they had no idea of our theory which alone explains that life. But they went as far as they could. It is the scientists who have gone that far already, who try to find room in the north for fertile land – as the only explanation of the facts which we have already cited – it is these scientists, we say, who will be the first to give their adherence to our theory. For it alone gives a logical explanation of the facts which they admit but cannot explain.

But at any rate, Dr. Tittman had no light to throw on Cook's claim except insofar as Cook reported neither open water nor fertile land, and in view of the unanimous discovery by explorers of open water in the regions of the polar orifice, it is very clear that Cook did not go as far north as he thought he went.

The Academy deserts Cook

And as a matter of fact when the Swedish Academy of Sciences and University of Copenhagen went over his alleged proofs they decided that he had not proved that he reached the pole. Of course, they were not in a position to state positively that he had not reached the pole, and Cook made much of the fact that their verdict was what he called 'neutral'. But the fact remains that they did not support him.

Cook admits he did not get there

And finally, we may note that in the book which Cook wrote to substantiate his claims, the book which he said would contain his case for the public's judgment, his final word, he himself admitted that he did not actually reach what is usually called the pole, but only approximated it. He says:

'Did I actually reach the North Pole? When I returned to civilization and reported that the boreal center had been attained, I believed that I had reached the spot toward which valiant men had strained for more than three hundred years . . . If I was mistaken in approximately placing my feet upon the pin-point about which this controversy has raged, I maintain that it is the inevitable mistake any man must make. To touch that spot would be an accident . . . Mr. Peary's case rests upon three observations of sun altitude so low that, as proof of a position, they are worthless.'

Peary's proof worthless

We may now glance at the sort of proof that Peary brought forward to substantiate his claim. In the first place, it is notable that he did not lose a minute in trying to discredit Cook. He had no sooner reached Labrador than he telegraphed home as follows:

'Cook was not at the North Pole on April 21, 1908, or at any other time. This statement is made advisedly.'

'Delayed by gale. Don't worry about Cook. Eskimos say Cook never left sight of land. Tribe confirms.'

And to the Associated Press he wired:

'Cook's story should not be taken too seriously. The two Eskimos who accompanied him say he went no distance north, and not out of sight of land. Other members of the tribe corroboate their story.'

And later:

'Do not trouble about Cook's story or attempt to explain any discrepancies in his statements. The affair will settle itself.

'He has not been at the pole on April 21st or any other time. He has simply handed the public a gold brick.

'These statements are made advisedly and I have proof of them. When he makes a full statement of his journey over his signature to some geographical society or other reputable body, if that statement contains the claim that he has reached the pole, I shall be in a position to furnish material that may prove distinctly interesting reading for the public.'

'Robert E. Peary.'

Peary also lacked witnesses

Of course one trouble with Cook's claim was that he had no witnesses of his deeds. The testimony of the

Eskimos was worthless for they knew nothing about making observations. But what was the surprise of the public to learn soon after this that Peary had no witnesses either.

In that interesting and very fair book on the subject of the polar controversy, *The Discovery of the North Pole*, being both Cook's and Peary's stories with an introduction by General Greely, edited by the Honorable J. Martin Miller, the editor says:

'Like Cook, Peary stood practically alone amid the desolation of "farthest north." Cook had with him two Eskimos who, as described by him, were panic-stricken and prayed to their deity. They were in no sense sharers of the emotion of their white master. And so it was with Peary, with the difference that his colored personal attendant was there to witness the triumph. One Eskimo – who was there – Egingwah by name – no doubt, looked on rather cynically at Peary's deeds...

'That Peary sent back all his white companions and pushed on alone to the pole caused a little surprise when first it became known. Yet it was recognized as just that the leader and inspirer of it should have all the glory. His were the risks; then why not his the honor? So, with bitter disappointment, perhaps, yet with unquestioning obedience to orders, the faithful companions of Peary stopped, one by one, within a few day's march of the pole and let him go ahead with his one swarthy companion.'

Now we cannot share the editor's sympathy with Peary in this matter. Not only had his companions shared his risks and thereby earned a part in the glory, but if Peary were not generous enough to acknowledge that, he ought to have seen the value of their corroborative evidence of his achievement. If Cook merely camped around for a few days barely out of reach of land, and then came back with a big claim, what was to prevent Peary simply going on a few miles ahead of his companions and then making a few observations, with nobody to verify them or check them up, and then come back and make any announcement he pleased?

Then Peary came back to civilization and it was found that several things about Cook's story which made it sound dubious were equally characteristic of Peary's story. He had taken even fewer observations of his alleged position at the Pole than Cook had done. Where Cook was doubted when he said he made fifteen miles a day in sledge traveling, Peary claimed to have made over twenty. As the Honorable Mr. Miller says:

'Peary was the only white man in his party to reach the pole . . . He alone made observations and reckonings at the pole. None of the men with him knew anything about determining latitudes or longitudes. They could not have known they had reached the pole unless Peary told them. Like Cook, Peary brought back practically his own word alone to support his claim that he had attained the earth's apex.

Peary's figures self-contradicting

'When we come to rate of travel, Cook's fifteen miles a day seems modest in comparison with the distance Peary covered. When near the eighty-eighth parallel, Peary decided to attempt to reach the pole in five days' marches. According to his story, he made twenty-five miles on the first day, twenty on the second, twenty on the third, twenty-five on the fourth and forty – yes, forty – on the fifth. On these last five days he traveled at an average rate of twenty-six miles a day.

'And on the return trip from the pole to Cape Columbia he made even better time. He tried, he says, on the return trip, to make double the distance he covered on his dash to the pole. "As a matter of fact," he declares, "we nearly did this, covering regularly on our return journey five outward marches in three return marches."

'It is easy to figure out the average rate of speed he

made on his return trip. He started back from the pole, he says, on April 7th and reached Cape Columbia on April 23, covering the 450 miles in sixteen days. This is a daily rate of 28.12 miles a day.

'Will the Arctic experts who declared it impossible for Cook to make fifteen miles a day charge Peary with falsehood when he says he made forty?'

One day, it will be remembered Peary actually claims to have made forty miles. Any reader who has been on a walking tour and knows what it is to walk forty miles a day on good roads with an inn to rest in at times, can tell what that would mean. Here was Peary, with his dogs to look after, his camp to make at night, his observations to make, his cooking to do, and certainly some repair work occasionally, making from twenty to forty miles a day. Oh but, the reader may exclaim, the dogs carried him along much faster than walking. But as a matter of fact they did not. Peary admitted that his pace was slower than walking – only he admitted it when he was not thinking of the bearing of the admission. It was when the newspaper men were interviewing him in Labrador. One of them, who did not know much about Arctic traveling asked:

'Did you ride?'

'Ride?' inquired the undaunted Peary, astonished. 'Sir, in Arctic expeditions a man is lucky if he is able to walk without pushing his sledge. Usually he may grip the rear and thrust it ahead. It is like guiding a breaking plow drawn by oxen. You must also expect at any moment that the sledge may strike some pressure ridge that will wrench you off your feet.'

So it comes to this: that in order to reach the so-called north pole a man must be able to do something as arduous as – and quite similar to – pushing a breaking plow drawn by oxen through Arctic ice at speeds varying from twenty to forty miles a day, and keep it up for eight days, after doing almost equally arduous work for months.

Miller thinks question insoluable

Is it any wonder that the Honorable Mr. Miller, after giving all this data sadly concludes that:

'The question whether Cook or Peary discovered the North Pole may never be solved. It bids fair to become one of history's conundrums, and to remain a matter of one man's word against another.'

But after all, Mr. Miller, if there is no pole to be discovered it is obvious that neither of your two heroes discovered it. The question will become relatively unimportant when we state it in its real form: Which of these men got furthest north? Surely that will not matter so much when we really explore the polar regions and find that what each man was after was simply a myth.

Now any doubt that we have thrown upon Peary's achievements by our words above is not a doubt raised by us alone. When Peary came to submit his proofs to investigation, the committee that went into the matter, afterwards acknowledged in congress that Peary had not, any more than Cook, proved his point.

Peary's own quotations show him up

How far he was from being able to prove it we may see by comparing some of his own statements. The following quotations were taken from Mr. Peary's own book, *The North Pole: Its Discovery, 1909*. We reproduce both the quotations and some comments that were made on them at the time the book was published:

'We turned our backs upon the pole at about four o'clock of the afternoon of April 7th.'

'According to a statement made on page 304, Mr. Peary took time on his return trip to make a sounding of the sea five miles from the pole.

'On page 305 Mr. Peary says: "Friday, April 9th, was a mild day. All day long the wind blew strong from the north-northeast, increasing finally to a gale." And on page 306, "We camped that night at eighty-seven degrees, forty-seven minutes."

'Mr. Peary thus claims to have traveled from the pole to this point, a distance of 133 nautical miles, or 157 statute miles, in a little over two days. This would average 76.5 statute miles a day. Could a pedestrian make such speed? During this time Mr. Peary camped twice, to make tea, eat lunch, feed the dogs, and rest – several hours in each camp.

'On page 310 Mr. Peary says: "We were coming down from the North Pole hill in fine shape now, and another double march, April 16–17, brought us to our eleventh upward camp at eighty-five degrees, eight minutes, one hundred and twenty miles from Cape Columbia."

'According to this, Mr. Peary covered the distance from eighty-seven degrees, forty-seven minutes, on April 9th, to eighty-five degrees, eight minutes, on April 17 – a distance of 149 nautical miles in eight days. This averaged twenty miles a day.

'On page 316 he says: "It was almost exactly six o'clock on the morning of April 23rd when we reached the igloo of Crane City at Cape Columbia and the work was done."

'Mr. Peary left eighty-five degrees, eight minutes, on April 17th, according to his statement, and traveled 120 miles to Cape Columbia in six days, arriving on April 23rd. This last stretch was at the rate of twenty miles a day. To sum up he traveled from the North Pole according to his statements, to land, as follows:

'The first 133 nautical miles southward in two days, at the rate of 66 nautical miles, or 7.5 satute miles, a day; the last 279 nautical miles in fourteen days, an average of twenty miles a day.

'According to Peary's book, Bartlett left him at eighty-seven degrees, forty-six minutes, and Mr. Peary started on his final spurt to the pole, a little after midnight on the morning of April 2nd. By arriving at the point where he left Bartlett on the evening of April 9th, he would have made the distance of 270 miles to the pole from this point and back, in a little over seven days.'

Mathew Henson's statements

'In the *New York World*, of October 3rd, 1910, page 3, column 6, Mathew Henson makes the following statement: "On the way up we had to break a trail, and averaged only eighteen to twenty miles a day. On the way back we had our own trail to within one hundred miles of land, and then Captain Bartlett's trail. We made from twenty to forty miles a day."

'At the rate of twenty miles a day on the way up, which Henson claims was made, it would have taken six days of twenty-four and eighteen hours to cover the distance of 135 miles from eighty-seven degrees, forty-seven minutes, to the pole. Adding the thirty-six hours Mr. Peary claims he spent at the pole for observations, eight days would have elapsed before they started back. Peary says the round trip of 270 miles from eighty-seven degrees, forty-seven minutes North to the pole, and the return to the same latitude, was done in seven days and a few hours.

'Why has Mr. Peary never been asked to explain his miraculous speed, and the discrepancy between his statement and Henson's?'

Congress in a dilemma

Well one may answer that by saying that as the Cook business had created one great international scandal, neither the authorities at Washington nor the American press were anxious to have another. One American had claimed that he had reached the pole. Foreign kings and princes had congratulated him, foreign universities had showered honors on him only to find out afterward that there was a great probability that they had been duped. If, following that, another American, an officer in the navy, had made a similar claim and that claim had been proved fraudulent, this country would not only have been the laughing-stock of the world but our national honor had been tarnished. Every American after that would have been regarded with suspicion. American scientists would be distressed. The United States would have been placed in an intolerable situation. Other nations would have pointed the finger of scorn at us, and our prestige would have been lowered all over the world.

Investigations a year later

No, Congress could not afford to make any public statement that Peary had played false or that he had even been honestly mistaken in his claim, for even a 'mistake' would have been made a matter of ridicule in the foreign press. So what was actually done? First a committee of the National Geographic Society was formed which rendered a favorable verdict after a cursory examination of Peary's field notes, and it was hoped that nothing more would happen. But something did happen. That verdict was challenged on the floor of Congress. A Congressional investigation was held a year later – when the clamor had died down – and its verdict was that Peary's proofs did not prove; that his achievement rested wholly upon his assertion – an assertion not backed up by a single white witness.

And the end of the story is just as significant. Great efforts were made by various parties to have the whole matter thrashed out, following the verdict of 'not proven' by the Congressional committee. But Congress and the government were afraid to act. Peary, significantly enough, never asked for an investigation and never replied to some very damaging charges brought against him not only by Cook but by independent societies. It was known that he wished to end his career after the polar exploit by retiring with the rank of Rear-Admiral – which carried a pension with it of $6,000. Friends of Peary brought into Congress a bill so retiring him. One would think that before such a reward was granted the charges would be pressed and Peary's claimed finding of the pole confirmed. But such was not to be. No inquiry was ordered. It is interesting to note that Professor Moore, president of the National Geographic Society which was financially interested in Peary's exploits, was one of the most active men in lobbying for this bill, and that he has since been dismissed from his position in the government service.

Summing up the lesson of this controversy

And what is the significant end to this story? It is that although the bill was signed it was changed before the signing took place, and the false assumption of Peary's 'Discovery of the Pole' was stricken out. That means that the government officially refused to endorse Peary although it could not afford to accuse him of anything that would lower us in the eyes of the world.

And there the matter rests. Neither Peary nor Cook had been able to prove that he reached the pole. Owing to the notorious difficulty in finding one's way around in a neighborhood where observations from the sun are not possible in winter – and the sun was barely above the horizon when both explorers were there – where distances are deceptive, where the compass is useless, where even Nansen admits he was absolutely lost – owing to all these difficulties we must not be astonished at the failure of these two men to find out where they really were. We need not even impute to them bad faith; both may have been honest in their claims although Peary's attacks on Cook and his failure to answer Cook's charges do reflect on him. But we cannot help noticing the difference in the reports of Arctic conditions which these two men make and those made by all previous explorers. Every previous investigator, who got really far north, found out the truth about the open polar sea and the rise of temperature as he neared the pole. The case for those two truths is bullet proof. Only Peary and Cook failed to see those two great facts, and in that failure we read the truth of their journeys – that they were not in the neighborhood of the polar orifice but at points further south than that. Had they gone further they would have found open water and increasing temperatures. Had they then possessed boats they could have launched on that sea and the way to the goal and to the truth would have been clear. They would have seen the earth's central sun shining even in the winter, shining all of the twenty-four hours and all of the year, and they would have discovered new continents and oceans, a new world of land and water and of forms of life some of which have vanished from the outside of the globe.

But it was not to be. The discovery of that new land was left to those who, following the theory outlined in this book, and using such safe means of Arctic traveling as the airplane or dirigible, will fly over the eternal barrier of ice to the warmer sea beyond and over that until they come into the realm of perpetual sunlight.

Gardner's book, now out of print and very difficult to find, was 450 pages in length. It included a bibliography of his research sources. After writing about Cook and Peary, he went on to build an impressive circumstantial case for a hollow earth. After publication, several newspapers across the country devoted full page feature stories to Gardner's idea. On Augst 3, 1913, *The Chicago Sunday Tribune* stated:

Marshall B. Gardner doese not say so in so many words that people live in the middle of the world. But he makes a circumstantial case to that effect. It is his belief that there is a big sun in the earth's interior, that there are immense holes where the poles are supposed to be, and that the phenomena of the aurora borealis and the aurora australis are the result of the interior sun shining through the polar holes.

'The Aurora man has spent years in studying out his theory. He asserts that the earth's interior, instead of being a molten mass of lava, as has been claimed by scientists for ages, is hollow and contains a central nucleus or material sun of about 600 miles in diameter.

Gardner declared the earth's crust was approximately 800 miles thick. The polar openings were 1,400 miles in diameter. The Illinoisan said that the mammoth originated inside the earth and these monstrous animals still live there. 'The huge carcasses that have been found frozen in arctic ice are not prehistoric,' he declared. 'These are animals that wandered out of the interior and froze after they reached the arctic.'

Right or wrong, Marshall B. Gardner was a remarkable man.

His book is proof of the twenty years of devotion to a fantastic cause.

TAMIL AND THE CAVE MASTERS

Through the ages, many occultists have retained a persistent belief in the Divine Masters. This is said to be a spiritual hierarchy, headed by ascended masters, who guide a dedicated band of loyal workers and initiates. Believers point to the myths and legends of many lands and cultures as proof of their belief. These tales report the manifestation of mysterious entities, or the appearance of unknown beings, during a critical moment in history. Some occultists claim these entities are messengers sent forth from the caves to guide surface civilization toward a spiritual path. Still others claim the caves are inhabited by the 'elders,' an older, more advanced, terrestrial race. The 'elders' moved underground when wild, sinful *homo sapiens* plotted to steal their higher knowledge.

Mrs. Margaret 'Maggie' Rogers, now deceased, came up with an astonishing story about two decades ago. She claimed to have spent three years in the caves as a guest of the Nephli, a benevolent race of advanced people. Mrs. Rogers claimed the Nephli moved into the caverns about the time Eve ate the apple and Mankind fell from Grace. She outlined her alleged experiences in several manuscripts and letters, claiming they were the secret teachings for a dawning New Age.

While redemption is one of the basic lessons of Christianity, it should be pointed out that Maggie Rogers was a heroin addict. In her own words, she was: '. . . an outcast . . . thirty-nine years old, a slave of drugs, pitted by smallpox, ugly, ragged,' and a beggar on the streets of Mexico City, Mexico.

Ex-addicts and drug experts have verified that many drugs create some pretty vivid hallucinations. Certain drugs extinguish the ability to tell what is real from what is fantasy or imagination. As an example, a user who takes a certain form of LSD will see a vivid purple haze. The mist shrouds the world like a psychedelic cloak. This type of LSD is known as 'purple haze acid,' and the haze is very real to a drugged user.

Mrs. Rogers' experience may have appeared real to her, yet it possibly did not occur. It may have been conjured up out of her drugged mind. Like everything else connected with the hollow earth mystery, Mrs. Rogers' material must be labelled as speculation. The reader must make his own decision on her story.

While she was in the caves, Maggie Rogers claimed to have read the Holy Scrolls of the Cave Masters, the *Hedon Rogia*. She claimed to have remembered the text after returning to the surface world. 'The Beginning' told the story of man's creation from the viewpoint of the creators. These were an advanced race of people who still remain in the state of grace.

Tamil, the Grand God of the Universe, reported that man is the off-spring of perfect people. Then, the Janza, a group of evil entities who use their powers in a negative manner, injected man with the seed of evil. After the earth was colonized, then it became necessary for the Nephli to go underground. The Janza were on the rampage again and their evil, negative acts endangered the Nephli. Using their advanced technology (like Shaver's Atlans and Titans), they constructed gigantic caverns and tunnels through the earth.

As the elder race migrated into the caves, a priest asked Tamil how long they would have to remain there.

'Through the ages,' Tamil answered. 'Yes, through the ages you will live below the surface, while wars and yet more wars rage above the ground. Again and again the will to war will devastate the earth; many nations will be obliterated. None will remember whence or why they vanished. Mankind will become as the beasts, with only a small spark of intelligence left. Little by little, he shall gain a foothold on the spiritual path, rising to great scientific heights, only to slide down again, rise again and slip again – through the ages it will be thus.'

'Will there be a sign to indicate when we can return from the caves?' asked the priest.

Tamil replied: 'When the fires break through the crust of the earth, when terrible new weapons are used by man to slay man, when parents and children slay each other, when mankind goes mad, when disease ravages the Earth and hunger slays those whom war has not slain, when the seas rise to erase entire cities, when Earth trembles and even the elements turn against man, then shall you know that the time is upon you and those whom you would have spared will know that the time is at hand. You will send envoys from time to time to choose worthy ones from the surface, namely those who have obeyed the laws of the Great One, and these you will allow to descend with their picked ones.

'Those elect whom you do not take with you shall be forewarned,' Tamil continued. 'They shall be told to go to a place of hiding which shall be for them alone. Then and only then will you know that the last great war is on you, that the sons of Janza are about to do battle with you for the last time, that man will be liberated for all time from the Evil One. When this war is ended, the world will be as Tamil meant it to be.'

While that isn't a very satisfying picture of the future, surface humanity can escape the catastrophes to come by following the lessons of the Nephli. Mrs. Rogers reported she brought these lessons back from the Cave Masters. They include:

Teaching of the Cave Masters

You will find that the cause of so much discord on your surface world is caused by intolerance.

Among the first ones, there were five different races from five planets. Those of the rose color were the giants, the Nephli, bidden by Tamil to lead these people to Earth.

If one of these was accursed, He would not have sent him to an earth He wanted to be an ideal place of habitation. Rest assured, then, that in the being of Tamil there is no partiality toward any race. He created us all, and intended that we should all be as brothers in our dealings.

You may have toiled manually or mentally; you may have risen to wealth by inheritance; yet you should never be a tyrant to those who serve you. A man who makes his servant his friend has in that one a faithful and loyal friend to whom he can come in time of stress. And is it not better to have the love of your servant than his hate?

Never pity yourself, nor consider yourself doomed to hell if you have the defects which all men hold, for you breed a little hell within yourself by so doing. You cannot go to the Nephli before you have learned even a little of their ways and teachings, and this takes patience. That is the main virtue. With it you learn not to rail at Tamil for things you have suffered because of your own defects. No, if you could only realize the fact that all the evil you now suffer is given you in order that you may more fully appreciate the good which will come to you later, you would find a state of peace easier and quicker.

Inasmuch as I, Tamil, have given you this earth to have and to hold from now on, I have also ordained that the race of Nephilium, *Paoles Geni* (reproductive race), shall lead you in the path that you shall tread. By kindness and example they shall lead you and teach you.

Do not worship me slavishly. Love me, but not because of fear.

You shall not take the life of your fellowman in the heat of passion.

Covet not that which your neighbor owns, neither mate, beast nor goods.

If your neighbor be gentle with you, be likewise. If unkind; turn away and see him not again.

Be careful in all you say, and criticize not your neighbor's way of life.

Abandon not your old ones, treat them gently; you too will come to that state.

Your life is not your own. Take it not, for I created it.

Take not by stealth from your fellowman that which is his.

Do not curse me, nor curse any other in my name, for it shall be as a boomerang and return unto you.

Honor the words of the elders, for they are of me and I speak through them.

Take no man or woman into bondage or slavery.

If your neighbor borrow grain from you and cannot repay due to crop failure, erase the debt, and I will erase your debt to me.

Cultivate patience, for in so doing you will find faith and peace.

I have given you life, intelligence, love and a body free from sin. Keep it so, lest the seed of Janza enter therein.

If evil be done you, seek not revenge, for I shall avenge you.

Never doubt that my love for you is that of a father, nor that I shall decide what is best for you.

Pray to me from your heart, not from a lesson learned by rote.

Ask not for the things that you need, for I shall supply them when the time is come.

Whine not, nor rail against your poverty, but see it as a lesson given you that you may learn to appreciate the good things to come.

Worship not false gods or idols, for if you cling to me, I will be all things to you and will demonstrate myself to, and through you.

Lie not heedlessly to me or to your fellowman. Yet if a lie is told by which you may save a friend from pain, it is forgiven even as it is told.

The Soul and Reincarnation

The body alone dies, not the soul. The soul goes to a place of 'choosing.' There it is scanned and tested, its record examined, and if it is found with a modicum of good, it is swept clean of all memory of its past before being sent back. This is done if its birth cycles have not been exhausted.

If that soul wishes to remain, but it has the seed of evil in it, it must undergo a period of atonement, purging, and cleansing in that world which humans call Purgatory; then, if it wishes, it may enter this world again with all debts paid.

If the soul is worn, rotten, and hopelessly impregnated with the seed of Janza to the exclusion of all good, it is put to an eternal sleep.

Every one of you who are on Earth now are there because you have not exhausted your cycles. You have been given the chance of redeeming yourselves. Earth is a punishment in itself.

Now the ka (Soul) has no sex. It has no passions of any kind. It is invisible, yet it is among us, mingling with its fellows on the stream of life. A child is born, and from that invisible life-stream the nearest ego to this child is swept into its tiny body and takes up its abode there. Maybe that ego in its past life was a male, yet it is swept into the body of a female. It has happened that two of these egos were swept into the same body at the same time. The result was what we call a bisexual or an invert. Therefore, they either love their own sex or they desire either of the two sexes.

Sex

You cannot master sex by suppressing it, but you must lift up the force. This you should do only if you have an excess of energy or when the urge comes upon you. Then do as we of the caves do:

Stand erect and let the air out of your lungs. When they are entirely empty, throw your head back as far as possible and inhale. Repeat this act several times. Now lie flat on the floor and raise the legs as high in the air as possible. Place the hands on the abdomen. Now raise your thoughts above all earthly matters or thoughts of bodily passion. Visualize a lovely land where all such things are unthought of; reflect on how foolish it is to let yourself be dominated by such things that have their own time and place in your life; for if these thoughts possess you, they smother the ethereal self. If you truly desire to become a person who lives for a higher life than this one, you should definitely decide to erase these things of the body, for it is absolutely necessary for one who would become a superbeing to have full control of his every sense.

Revelations from the Cave Masters

Do not slight as unimportant the revelations which are shown to you, for a message may be given you even in a dream. Sometimes these dreams are distorted, but if you study them carefully, you will realize that many of them contain memories of the past. We appear to you many times this way, and we try to teach you through the medium of dreams. We do this when we cannot contact you through telepathy. We never send evil impulses, so keep alert and on the lookout for these dreams and thoughts.

In past ages we talked to you, and you heard us and knew it was we who spoke, for your acts vary little during various lives. They follow more or less the same pattern. You may doubt reincarnation, but if you are just and probe deeply, you will be forced to admit that it is true.

Many of you have had a certain vision which I can repeat, even to the minor details. You are in a seemingly endless tunnel; you are so tired and you have grown hopeless of ever emerging. You go on and on, and at last, you see a tiny light far away. Then after a long time, you see the end of the tunnel and hasten toward it. You finally emerge into a peaceful valley, gorgeous with flowers and lit by a lavender sun. Now your tired feet no longer trudge along. You begin to float. On and on you go until at last you see the Rock, the Altar, with its flat top, on which stands the figure of a giantess. She is clad in a blue and silver robe. She is the High Priestess. You know instinctively that those large white hands are healing hands. You look at the serenity and the beauty around you, and there comes to you a great desire to stay in that place forever. Even when you awake you feel nostalgia for that land.

Predictions of future disasters

Already you have noticed that the climate is changing. Unrest and fear are riding the world. Earth tremors are prevalent; many die by fire; fatal accidents take many lives; floods sweep over the lands; and many are the victims of senseless slayings. The seed of Janza, which lies in many of you, has budded and bloomed and is about to bear bitter fruit.

The age-old prophecy says thus: 'And in the last days of the dominance of the rebels on the earth, there shall be many disasters. The seas shall return to their original beds, and where they now lie shall be gardens and deserts as of old. One more great war shall come, and many shall be the bodies which shall perish. The nations of the world shall seek haven under the earth. The *Ka* of the slain ones shall go to the last place of choosing and from there to rebirth or to eternal life. That small last spot of rottenness shall be cut out from the soul of man, and he shall be given a new body if he wishes. But those in whom the rot has spread until no trace of white is seen shall be obliterated as though they had never been.'

Janza will come to grips with the hosts of the earth, and they shall be on the verge of losing to him, yet the Nephilium will arise in all their might and power, and they will defeat him and all his hordes forever. Many of you will see that last great struggle, and those who believe in Tamil's divine goodness will, because of your faith, walk through it all and not a thread of your clothing shall be destroyed nor a hair of your heads harmed.

A Message for Surface Man

Study these words thoroughly and note them well; check them against future events as they occur, for they are omens of the great changes to come.

'And a mist shall arise, the mist which slays, which is formed from the doubts, fears, and hatred of man. To breathe it is fatal, for all those petty hates, demonic thoughts and ideas shall gather together and form that white mist which is pure poison. This mist shall tarnish as it travels, and it will travel from the west to the east, and wherever it lingers or even passes, all life shall cease and fade away. The catastrophe is close upon us. As the tower of Babel fell, not because those who erected it could, by any remote chance, have reached to Heaven, but because mankind aspired to reach Heaven for no good motive, and because man aspired to conquer Heaven itself, all evil forces shall be gathered together in an effort to erase man from the face of the earth. There will indeed be weeping and wailing and gnashing of teeth. That mist, engendered of man's own hates and malice, shall return upon him, even as a boomerang returns to the hand of him who casts it, and when all hope seems lost, those Great Ones who are destined to save the remnant of humanity shall come forth to overcome Janza.'

A princeling was born some years ago in a far-off land

and exchanged for a newly-born surface child so that he might be raised as such and learn all he needed to know of man. Soon he will be taken away again to the caves, and the memory of his past lives will be given to him so that he may know his duty in the days to come. When this is finished, he will come as a being of Light and Glory in order that all man may know that He is the true Son of Tamil. He will be endowed with Godlike qualities, which will enable him to rule in wisdom and in love and to restore to the world the harmony that existed when the world was first colonized.

You who have sought for so long shall find that which you seek, for your eyes will at last be opened to the fact that all the past histories of the world are written in the stones, and man shall see and comprehend them. Can you not see that nothing ever really dies? We speak, we laugh and sing, and all is recorded on the etheric waves. The vestiges of a lost race and a lost continent will carry new meaning for you.

Your present inventions are great in your eyes, but you have only scratched the surface. You ask for our science, but your minds are still too small to use it wisely. Gold is still your God, a god with which to torture your fellowman. If we permitted, you of the surface world would wrest our treasures from us, and some one man would rise to power and seek to become king of the world. That cannot be, for we will use our power not to subdue the world and rule it by fear, but to establish a rule of peace and equality.

Enlightenment is coming to all of you who have studied our ways, and you realize it becouse of the phenomena we are showing you. We do not ask, nor yet expect, that you be as perfect as Tamil and the High Ones are; for after all, you are flesh and blood and the flesh is weak. Had Tamil expected you to be perfect. He never would have made you as He did, with only a spark of the Divine.

Tamil, is a gentle father, and even as an earthly father. He makes allowance for your misdeeds. If you are so weary at nightfall that when you lie down to rest you fall asleep before you can pray to Him, He does not curse you.

Many of you flagellate yourselves needlessly. Your will power to overcome temptation is known also to Him and to us, as is your will to learn, so that in days to come you will be able and willing to pass along your knowledge to others who may wish to learn.

The time has not yet come when you will have reached the peak, but when it does, you will be inspired to teach and to do it well. When you have studied these lessons well, even if your destiny is not that of a healer, you will still be able to heal with a touch of your hand, or to heal mental burdens with a word of comfort.

Beware of pride and vanity lest they rule you, for these things will kill whatever talent you possess. The calm you will have cultivated will carry you through any ill.

In the last days the world will be more troubled than ever before. Man will slay man in one gigantic struggle. You may tell those who wish to know of these things, but if they jeer, say no more, for they are hopeless and their brains are asleep. Live without fear, for naught may harm you, as the chosen mentors are with you, and they care for your chosen ones as well. When destruction is widespread, look to Him with eyes of faith so that He may know you are confident of His protection.

Again I say, when the seasons change, the animals die from unknown causes, and the earth shakes, have no fear, for you will be invincible and ready for entrance into our world.

We are almost ready to come. Already our craft rides high above the storm clouds. The dial is set, and the clock's hands are racing toward the hour when you will be called. Make your peace with those whom you have ill-treated, and be ready, for the time is short. Go openly to those whom you have sinned against and win their forgiveness. Right all wrongs possible in these last days so that no man may hate you and wish you ill.

Also available from Sphere Books

GODS AND SPACEMEN IN ANCIENT ISRAEL

W. RAYMOND DRAKE

If spacemen are really visiting Earth today, as world-wide sightings suggest, the wonders of the New Testament show that they surely also influenced men in the days of early Christianity, which, in its essence, taught a cosmic religion to be shaped by peoples of all the planets. Should science succeed in dismissing extraterrestrial influence on Earth, the same logic would deny the existence of Jesus and imply that Christianity was based upon a myth. W. Raymond Drake offers startling evidence about the ancestry of Jesus, the raising of the pyramids, the building of Solomon's Temple, and the destruction of Sodom and Gomorrah by nuclear attack.

0 7221 3034 1 65p

GODS AND SPACEMEN IN GREECE AND ROME

W. RAYMOND DRAKE

The greatest writers of antiquity agree that once there was a wonderful Golden Ast on earth ruled by 'gods'. It was destroyed by wars and cataclysm, and Man degenerated through the Silver and Bronze Ages to our own Iron Age. Were the 'gods' who helped the city of Athens defeat the invading armies of Atlantis visitors from other planets? Was the beautiful Helen of Troy a space queen? Were the flying shields which helped Alexander the Great storm the walls of Tyre spacecraft? W. Raymond Drake argues that these and other supernatural phenomena add up to real evidence that a race with advance knowledge was at work in the classical world.

0 7221 3046 5 75p

GODS AND SPACEMEN IN THE ANCIENT WEST

W. RAYMOND DRAKE

North American Indians worshipped a Great Spirit in the sky who descended to Earth in human form to teach warriors and heal the sick. In Mexico the Aztecs surrendered themselves to the Conquistadores, believing them to be the White Gods, returning to earth like Quetzalcoatl of long ago. From the Arctic to the Amazon, the legends of ancient American civilizations tell of White Gods from the stars who once ruled in a Golden Age on earth. Investigating these legends, W. Raymond Drake advances the startling theories of his other books and offers new explanations for the fascinating lands and legends of the 'New World'.

0 7221 3045 7 45p